BODY CONNECTIONS

Michael S. Koppel

BODY CONNECTIONS

BODY-BASED SPIRITUAL CARE

Abingdon Press
Nashville

BODY CONNECTIONS:
BODY-BASED SPIRITUAL CARE

Copyright © 2021 Abingdon Press

All rights reserved.

No part of this work may be reproduced or transmitted in any form or by any means, electronic or mechanical, including photocopying and recording, or by any information storage or retrieval system, except as may be expressly permitted by the 1976 Copyright Act, the 1998 Digital Millennium Copyright Act, or in writing from the publisher. Requests for permission should be addressed in writing to Permissions, Abingdon Press, 2222 Rosa L. Parks Blvd., Nashville, TN 37228-1306, or emailed to permissions@abingdonpress.com.

Library of Congress Control Number: 2021942001
ISBN: 978-1-7910-1341-7

Scripture quotations unless noted otherwise are from the Common English Bible. Copyright © 2011 by the Common English Bible. All rights reserved. Used by permission. www.CommonEnglishBible.com.

Scripture quotations noted NRSV are from the New Revised Standard Version Bible, copyright © 1989 National Council of the Churches of Christ in the United States of America. Used by permission. All rights reserved worldwide. http://nrsvbibles.org/

21 22 23 24 25 26 27 28 29 30—10 9 8 7 6 5 4 3 2 1
MANUFACTURED IN THE UNITED STATES OF AMERICA

*In gratitude for the friendship of
Bill O'Donnell (October 5, 1964–August 19, 1987),
whose body story ended far too soon.*

This book is dedicated in his honor and memory.

Contents

Introduction: The Dream Inside	1
Chapter 1. Our Body Story	9
Chapter 2. Becoming Body Conscious	25
Chapter 3. Staying with Our Bodies	43
Chapter 4. Focusing as Healing Practice	65
Chapter 5. Sensing the Sacred	81
Chapter 6. Silent Prayer through Our Bodies	99
Chapter 7. God's Armor and Our Bodies	123
Chapter 8. Humanizing Bodies: Exposing and Transforming Stories	141
Chapter 9. Conclusion: Being Home	161
Bibliography	175
Subject Index	183
Scripture Index	187
Acknowledgments	189

Introduction

THE DREAM INSIDE

"Who will help you excavate the dream hiding inside you?" asks songwriter Jesse Palidofsky.[1] Jesse's song reminds us that the dream hides within us. Close to our experience and within our bodies, we meet God, too. In our time, "the informational queries of *who* and *what* [is God], along with their authoritative answers have been traded for the experiential and open-ended concerns of *where* and *how*."[2] Where and how do I discover myself and God?—that is the question this book explores. We can discover, in part, by uncovering our God-inspired identity and sharing this gift with the world. The dream of who we are and what we are called to become gets covered with layers of doubt, confusion, brokenness, disappointment, grief, and pain. We know difficult life experiences can grind us down emotionally and physically, leaving us depleted and exhausted. Life gets buried within us. We yearn for a way to get back in touch with God, our true selves, and others. We can tap into the dream and call upon its energy for our lives as we learn the faith practice of digging. We do this by paying attention, asking daring faith questions, and exploring unfamiliar and avoided territory. We cast aside the dirt that buries live energy struggling to breach the surface.

Our bodies hold the dream, yet they can become weighed down by life burdens. Jesus teaches: "Follow me, and let the dead bury their own dead"

---

1. "Dancing Toward the Light," Azalea City Recordings, 2014.

2. Diana Butler Bass, *Grounded: Finding God in the World—A Spiritual Revolution* (San Francisco: HarperOne, 2015), 1.

(Matt 8:22). It is a call to lighten our load by focusing on what matters in response to God in the journey of discovery. At core is the encouragement not to put energy into lifeless things. We cannot undo the past, but we can engage in practices individually and collectively to lessen its hold on us and live toward a hopeful future. To acknowledge regrets, wounds, and transgressions, among other experiences, allows for the possibility of change and newfound freedom for our bodies. King David mourns the death of his son birthed by Bathsheba in 2 Samuel 12:15ff. Through grief, his body reckons with the choices that have contributed to this fateful moment. The past cannot be undone. Through grief, though, his body finds release. We follow God's call and our own longing by letting go of the past that weighs us down. We let the dead bury the dead by letting go of our preoccupations and charting a path toward justice and peace. We tap and work toward the transformation of root fears that keep us and others from living into the future God intends. Uncovering the dream inside entails facing what haunts us and holds us back, which can be daunting. Layer by layer we learn to shift inwardly toward God's shalom. We can choose to partner with our bodies, the often neglected and forgotten companion in our faith journey.

We practice empathy with our own and others' bodies through "experience-near observation."[3] We stop, rest, notice, and reflect on circumstances within and around our bodies. This is what a good therapist would do while listening to our story. We can learn to do this gently with our bodies. We don't plow through but instead stay open to learning. We say, "Something is going on here" and "I want to look into it." This approach feels expansive. It is the difference between gently brushing aside the dirt to reveal an ancient artifact or using a hammer and chisel to reveal the same.

I have learned the importance of listening with the body. As a pastor and teacher steeped in theory, I am sometimes more comfortable starting "in my head." My own body work has helped make me more in tune with the bodies of others. While teaching a class for hospital chaplains who

---

3. See Allen M. Siegel, *Heinz Kohut and the Psychology of the Self* (New York: Routledge, 1996), 105, 170.

serve the military and veterans, I noticed weariness on their faces. They looked how my body felt. One morning after several intensive days of class, I awoke with what I would describe as knots in my back, a familiar place of tension. Then I listened to the word going through my head: pay attention to the "nots." I had been focused on what was *not* happening, what seemed *not* to be right, how the connections between theory and practice were *not* being made. It was a long list of "nots" and I was holding myself responsible. As I acknowledged the mental litany of "nots," I could sense the *easing of the knots* in my back. I started class the following day by encouraging class members to ease their knots by making connections between their bodies and what was occurring in their lives and ministries.

We need help to reclaim body knowledge. This book serves as a guide. God's love embraces our wholeness—body, mind, spirit—but we often leave the body out. We walk around, heads disconnected from bodies, mindlessly hurting each other and unable to heal. We need to surface into awareness what has been lost or forgotten. We do not just *have* bodies; we *are* bodies. In Genesis 2:7, God breathes into 'adam the breath of life and 'adam becomes a living body/being. Here's the rub: people have taken this to support a division of body and soul, mind, and spirit. The *unity* of the *living being* in Genesis 2:7 cautions against separation.[4]

Trusting Bodies

People say, trust yourself. But we may be unsure how to do it. We know trust develops in the earliest years of life and forms the basis for faith in God. We learn to trust in relationship with caring mothers/fathers/caregivers who provide actual "holding" and the "total environmental provision" that supports our life and growth.[5] When we create a safe, welcoming space for other people to express feelings and thoughts, we offer a hospitable holding environment. This space of welcome sends a message: you

---

4. Denise Dombkowski Hopkins argues against reading this passage as "a metaphysical, ethical dualism" that in effect would make the body inferior to the mind and spirit. See Rodney J. Hunter, ed., *Dictionary of Pastoral Care and Counseling* (Nashville: Abingdon Press, 2005), 87.

5. D. W. Winnicott, *The Maturational Processes and the Facilitating Environment* (Madison, CT: International Universities Press, 1988), 43–46.

are recognized and valued here. Our bodies and sense of self in life's early stages need reliable and consistent care in order to develop. We don't need perfect caregivers or a perfect environment; they just need to be "good enough" so we have space to learn and grow from failures and mistakes.[6]

We create holding environments for others because we care. Caring for our own bodies is a way of creating a "holding environment" for ourselves. We do this by cultivating an attitude of consistent respect for whatever we experience. We don't put ourselves or others down. Caring for our bodies is faithful moral activity in a world that fragments, torments, and traumatizes. If we are blessed to have a "good enough" life, then we are strengthened for when life pushes us over. For those who have experienced frayed and damaging early relationships, the work of building trust is even more pressing.

Our capacity to trust our experience and our bodies helps us navigate life trauma. We take steps toward trust for ourselves and for the benefit of others since we never know how or when we will encounter the aftershocks of trauma. What impact does trauma have on spiritual seekers and religious adherents who want to live a faithful life? Even without our realization, we are all immersed in trauma at different levels and to various degrees. Trauma is a complex emotional response to a real or perceived threat to our life. Traumatic responses can even occur in an encounter with what Phyllis Trible calls "texts of terror."[7] These texts include: the use, abuse, and banishment of Hagar and her son Ishmael (Gen 16:1-6; 21:8-21); Tamar being raped by her half-brother, Amnon (2 Sam 12:1-22); and the rape and dismemberment of the unnamed woman (Judges 19). These Bible stories of horror require interpretation "of outrage on behalf of their female victims in order to recover a neglected history, to remember a past that the present embodies, and to pray that these terrors shall not come to pass again."[8] Trust informs our ability to declare, "Something isn't right here." We need to heed that message for ourselves and on behalf of others.

---

6. Winnicott, *The Maturational Processes and the Facilitating Environment*, 145–46.

7. Phyllis Trible, *Texts of Terror: Literary-Feminist Readings of Biblical Narratives* (Minneapolis: Fortress, 1984).

8. Trible, *Texts of Terror*, 3.

Introduction

When I served as a campus minister, I led a Bible study with a group of young adults including singles and married people from a local congregation. Together we reflected on Genesis 22, the story of Abraham sacrificing Isaac. Emily, a young mother in the group, had a strong visceral response to the story. "How could Abraham possibly do that?" she exclaimed. She was aware of revulsion coursing through her body. Her intense body agitation signaled a protest to the story: "This should not be! How could a parent sacrifice his own son?"

Emily's exclamation comes from being in touch with her body. Other group members initially wanted to ignore or rationalize Emily's response. We all benefited, though, from creating space so we, too, could listen along with Emily's body response. It provided a clue for how we can all learn to *read with our bodies*. When we ignore, lose touch with, and rationalize body messages, we separate ourselves from a vital resource. Judith Herman, in her groundbreaking work on recovery from trauma, notes: "Safety always begins with the body. If a person does not feel safe in her body, she does not feel safe anywhere. Body-oriented therapies, therefore, can be useful in early recovery."[9] When we listen and read with our bodies, we are engaged in moral activity: discerning between what is healing and right and what is damaging and wrong. As a physician at a conference once said to me, we need to pay heed to eating, drinking, sleeping, and exercise. It seems simple, he emphasized. We complicate matters by thinking there is something wrong with us when the body presents uncomfortable information. We need to listen to the messenger!

Caring for our bodies is proactive spiritual practice. We may find ourselves right now in offensive mode, a plateau of time that affords space to pay attention to our body experience. We may find ourselves in defensive mode, a pinched place in which we need to adapt and respond so that we do not harm others or ourselves. Regardless of where we find ourselves, this book helps us partner with our bodies as we encounter stress and trauma in life, in faith communities, and in reading Bible stories.

---

9. Judith Herman, *Trauma and Recovery: The Aftermath of Violence—From Domestic Abuse to Political Terror* (New York: Basic Books, 2015), 269.

Introduction

God Loves the Body

Our bodies situate us in the world that God loves. We are like "all others, some others, and no other."[10] Our identities are connected to bodies. Selfhood can seem abstract, but "bodyhood" is not. It seems almost silly to use this language, but it highlights an important point: self-reference is also body reference. We need to include the body in conversation, not exclude it. We need to say to ourselves "my body is part of who I am." Since knowledge is power, we want to harness body knowledge for becoming God's beloved bodies in the world. I describe myself and my body as follows: Protestant, contemplative, middle-class, Caucasian, educated, able-bodied, swimmer, hiker, biker, singer, male, minister, and professor. We own our body location because we are always "insider" to our personal experience and "outsider" to the experience of others. In the pages of this book, I write as an insider, attempting to describe my internally lived and embodied experience. I invite readers to pay attention to their embodied experience and to cultivate curiosity for the similarities and differences with others. Such a posture of internal attunement and external observation embodies healing spiritual care practice. God loves the world, which includes our bodies. We pay attention to our own bodies, and to those of others, to partner with God in care for the world.

Several intersecting definitions of "body" emerge in this book. They include the body as: **physiology**, the living and functioning organism of being human; **metaphor**, a network of associations, of learning about a lesser-known through a better-known integrated and interrelated whole; **location of experience**, the vehicle in and through which life is encountered; **storyteller**, expresses narratives through its own language and symbol system; and **bearer of relationship**, created in and for connection with others. Caregiving and spiritual practice are enriched by the complex meanings and associations of the term.

The book unfolds in nine chapters. Chapter 1, "Our Body Story," explores our bodies as storytellers in pastoral and spiritual care. Chapter 2, "Becoming Body Conscious," outlines steps for becoming participant

---

10. Emmanuel Y. Lartey, *In Living Color: An Intercultural Approach to Pastoral Care and Counseling*, 2nd ed. (London: Jessica Kingsley, 2003), 31–22.

observers with change. Chapter 3, "Staying with Our Bodies," shows how to partner with our bodies through anxiety and transition. Chapter 4, "Focusing as Healing Practice," develops the practice of "focusing" to get in touch with our body story. Chapter 5, "Sensing the Sacred," reflects on body senses in caring connection with God and with one another. Chapter 6, "Silent Prayer through Our Bodies," considers the healing effects of prayer and meditation with the body. Chapter 7, "God's Armor and Our Bodies," suggests proactive steps for protective body care for ourselves and with others in contexts of trauma. Chapter 8, "Humanizing Bodies," exposes the harm of keeping secrets and offers practices for transforming body stories. Chapter 9, "Being Home," offers body practices for making our home in the world.

Here's an image for living freely as God's beloved. On a late spring morning, I glanced out the back window of my house to the lush green backyard. My eye caught the sudden movement of what seemed like a branch falling from a large maple tree. I heard a thud and noticed a small bundle scamper away. A squirrel had just fallen from a tree limb high above, gotten up, and run back up the tree trunk. Not all squirrels survive all tree falls. But most survive most of the time because squirrels have adapted. They instinctually know to use their bodies and tails for adjustment. What can we learn from the natural environment about adaptability and flexibility in the body? We learn to open to resistance, stay flexible, get up, and try again. This is a way to develop resilience.

A physician friend reflects on the relationship between our bodies and spirituality: "People tend to develop illnesses when there is disconnection between who they think they are and who they truly are." This insight is not meant to be judgment on those who develop illnesses but merely an observation. It is also not a declaration of cause-and-effect relationship. Such a statement can prompt a knowing nod of agreement or an angry response. But at the very least it calls for deeper reflection on the choices we make in life. Not all disease results from our choices. People with lung cancer are not always smokers who could be blamed for their choice to smoke. Colorless and odorless radon gas is known to cause lung cancer. Not every family can afford radon abatement. Food deserts in cities limit healthy food choices that lead to development of diabetes and hypertension. Personal choices have been minimized by systemic inequality. To the extent that we can make healthy choices, we need to do so without judging those who do not have those choices available to them. It is social and economic structures that need to be called to account.

Our bodies help us identify and embrace our God-inspired purpose, the dream calling forth within us. May we manifest the dream and follow where it leads.[11] We are invited as individuals and communities to explore partnership with our bodies, to foster healing practices, and to work toward the removal of barriers that cause bodies to suffer. Time is fleeting. We can act now.[12]

Body Care Prayer

On our journey
    Connect us, O Holy One,
        In
            Body
Heal wounds.
Mend divisions.
Open us anew.
Amen.

---

11. Duane R. Bidwell suggests that short-term and long-term spiritual direction takes a "dual focus" by "identifying God's action and discerning appropriate response." See *Short-Term Spiritual Guidance* (Minneapolis: Augsburg Fortress, 2004), xii.

12. This parallels the spiritual approach that many church members as well as the "nones" desire: "a practical theology of immanent transcendence . . . that focuses on the concrete reality of the here-and-now." See Elizabeth Drescher, *Choosing Our Religion: The Spiritual Lives of America's Nones* (New York: Oxford University Press, 2016), 248, emphasis added.

Chapter 1
OUR BODY STORY

"Have a seat and you'll see how it is." That was Nancy's invitation to the dean. As a child, Nancy contracted polio that affected her whole body. She could walk only short distances with a leg brace.

Nancy depended mostly on maneuvering by wheelchair. By 1987, before the historic passage of the Americans with Disabilities Act in 1990, the Yale Divinity School had made some necessary changes to its building to accommodate students, staff, and faculty. But there still were no electric door openers.

The dean had a seat in Nancy's chair. He quickly realized how difficult it was to open and move through the narrow doors in a wheelchair, even for an able-bodied person with two fully functioning arms. For Nancy, it was impossible. While useable with a brace, her one arm was by no means strong enough to open a door while seated. It required two people to maneuver through the doors—one person to open and to hold the door and another person to push the chair.

Soon after the dean's ride in Nancy's wheelchair, electric openers were installed on the doors.

Every*body* has a story. Nancy is a gifted minister, beloved and appreciated by the churches and communities she has served. Her life story is more than a description of what her body can and cannot do. Nancy's body story is hers. We have our own. When the dean sat in Nancy's chair, he faced obstacles that Nancy confronted on a regular basis. Sitting in the chair taught him a bit about Nancy's body story. When we "take a seat" in our own experience, we allow our bodies to show us our way in faith.

Our body story has many dimensions. Some aspects of the story are known only to us while other aspects can be observed by other people. Some aspects of our body story are known in and through relationship with others. Our body story changes over time and finds wholeness through connection to God's creation story. Tuning in to our body story is sacred work. We might initially be uncomfortable thinking this way. But gradually as you tune in more frequently, you will likely discover God's mystery unfolding all around.

Charles Wesley, hymnwriter and brother of John Wesley, founder of the Methodist movement, in a prayer for children urged: "Unite the pair so long disjoined, Knowledge and vital piety: Learning and holiness combined."[1] The prayer is noteworthy for its adult viewpoint. As adults, we pray that children will join faith and learning in their lives. We assume they already know how to inhabit their bodies and to engage in play! As we grow into adulthood, we can lose touch with the natural delight our bodies offer for engaging in God's creation. Mature faith calls for a return to embodied knowing. We reconnect with our bodies through *attention* and *intention* since God reveals God's self in and through our bodies. Body theology is not the work of academic theologians alone, but it belongs to each of us. Body theology is "nothing more, nothing less than our attempts to reflect on body experience as revelatory of God."[2]

Attention is an inward and outward practice. As we bring attention inward (inner attunement), we are more likely to manifest a calm attentive presence. Dance critic Sarah Kaufman calls this form of social composure "grace": "an essential, treasured quality, which ought to be at the heart of how we interact, how we inhabit our bodies and the world around us."[3] "At its essence, grace is the transference of well-being from one who is calm and comfortable" to others.[4] For Christians, grace refers to God's forgiving and releasing love for us. God's grace continually works in and

---

1. Charles Wesley, "Hymn XL," in *Hymns for Children* (Bristol: E. Farley, 1763). Reprinted by Gale Eighteen Century Collections Online Print Editions.

2. Sallie McFague, *The Body of God: An Ecological Theology* (Minneapolis: Fortress, 1992), 44.

3. Sarah L. Kaufman, *The Art of Grace: On Moving through Life* (New York: W. W. Norton, 2016), xv.

4. Kaufman, *The Art of Grace*, xvii.

through us to restore us to full relationship with God, our neighbors, and ourselves. We are called to live both kinds of grace: as a social skill and as a theological practice. We listen to our body stories as a means to be in touch with what is actually happening and in order to participate with God toward the ushering in of shalom, peace, and well-being.

Shifting Our Attention

As an accomplished professional leader, Rebecca returned to graduate school to follow the tugging call to ministry she had sensed for a while. In class, I noticed her sitting at the table with arms crossed close to her body and a shawl wrapped across her shoulders. I kept the observation to myself. During a class discussion toward semester's end, someone asked about my sabbatical writing project, and I talked briefly about my desire to help people contemplate and engage care practices with the body. At that point, the student commented, "That's very interesting. You might be wondering why I sit this way, kind of hugging my body. Well, it was a way to make me feel solid when I so often felt disembodied in the household in which I grew up."

We begin wherever we are with body care. Beginning includes naming how we see our body relationship.[5] How we see this relationship informs how we act. Consider these possibilities: (1) battlefield: "where good and evil are pitted against each other, and the forces of light battle the forces of darkness": we experience our bodies as a place of conflict, tension, and hostility; (2) trap: "to disentangle and escape from [the messiness]": we experience our bodies as a place that needs to be avoided for fear of becoming caught up; (3) lover: "beheld as intimate and gratifying partner": we experience our bodies as a partner in affection and appreciation; (4) self: "union springs from a deep knowing": we experience our bodies as a source of wisdom.[6] Other ways to view our bodies include partner, friend, antagonist, burden, and alien. What does the image you choose suggest positively and/or negatively about your relationship to your body? What feelings come to the surface as you reflect on your image?

---

5. Joanna Macy, *World as Lover, World as Self* (Berkeley, CA: Parallax, 1991), 4.
6. See Macy, *World as Lover, World as Self*, 5–11, bold added.

Chapter 1

> **Starting Point Questions:** How would you describe the relationship with your body? If none of the four categories listed above reveal the relationship, what category would you add? How have your views of your body changed over time?

We generate self-talk that spins around in our heads. Self-talk is self-generated and self-preoccupied thought that offers ongoing commentary on anything and everything in our lives. The self-talk or story lines get in the way of our experiencing the fullness of life that God intends. These story lines of self-talk are often self-limiting and negative, as in, "I don't measure up," "I'm not good enough," "I need to please," "I must follow the rules," "I can't make my own decisions," or "I don't know what I want." We need to practice interrupting ourselves! "Just stop it!" as comedian Bob Newhart urged in a skit when playing a psychiatrist on an episode of *MADtv*. We need to investigate the story lines because they interfere with God's story of love. What do we do with the self-generated and often negative story lines? Drop them and practice being with whatever sensations, experience, or feelings manifest in the body. Here is where our worldview comes into play. If we are at war with the world, it is likely to manifest in the body as anger and frustration. Negative thoughts and emotions encase us in anxiety and fear (trapped mentality). Or else thoughts may provoke conflict with others because we feel torn or at war in our bodies (battlefield mentality). We have to explore for ourselves how our relationship to our bodies activates positive and negative body responses for us and others. We probably sense that replaying our mental story line does not change anything and holds the body hostage to the endless loops. We feel caught with no escape. Being with the anger and frustration or whatever is experienced in the body opens the way for change. As we drop the story and stay with the energy in the body, we might notice new possibilities for ourselves. We listen to our body's story and not just the chatter in our heads.

> **Questions for Reflection:** What self-story loop do you mentally replay? How does this affect your body?

We cannot rationalize ourselves into a new way of living. Our attempts to do so leave us feeling frustrated. Mental "spinning of wheels" leaves imprints on the body in the form of anger, frustration, and tension. When we encounter these unwanted visitors, we may not know what to do. We might ignore, run away, or fight. Each of these actions comes from a place of fear and hostility, and in effect, minimizes or negates our bodies for sending the message. We subjugate our bodies by "blaming the victim," replicating dynamics between abusers and the abused.

> **Exercise in Body Connection:** Stop and take stock. Receive and believe what the body tells you without covering it over, making excuses, or pressing forward. This is an exercise with our own bodies as if they have been abused, harmed, or neglected. Proceed with caution: people who have direct experience with emotional, physical, psychological, or spiritual abuse may need to consult with professionally trained counselors.
>
> Ask body-oriented questions. What is occurring within my body right now, and how might it relate with what is happening in my life with family, friends, work, and the wider community?

As we begin to embrace wholeness, we grow in trusting ourselves and we learn to question negative story lines that cause harm. Interestingly, in Buddhism, there is an emphasis on not simply believing truth handed down from others. People must come to see truth for themselves. Searching for true reality depends on self-trust and an ability to see through illusions and deceptions. This teaching is also helpful for Christians. If we buy into the negative story lines about ourselves, then we do not stand on the solid ground of trust. It is hard to be open to grace. If we are true to who God has created us to be and to the story we are called to live out, then we cannot deny our body story and body experience. Nor can we repeat what may be true for others but not true for ourselves. We embrace our wholeness by believing and trusting our body experience.

> **Reflection Point:** Call to mind a recent experience when you sensed agitation, conflict, or tension in your body. As you reflect now, consider how embracing the truth your body revealed helps you revise a negative story line about yourself or others.

Chapter 1

Healing Rhythms

As Christians, we say the body is central to faith because we believe God has become flesh in Jesus Christ. However, we are often more comfortable talking about God's Holy Spirit. We are not always sure what to do with our bodies. We do not want to idolize the body, but neither do we want to denigrate it. Jesus's body story and God's order of creation can point us toward healing.

Christ's body story teaches us to live into fullness and emptiness. *Fullness* is about embracing our body-selves, and *emptiness* is about offering body-selves. Consider these reflections from scripture. On fullness: "The Word became flesh and made his home among us. We have seen his glory, glory like that of a father's only son, full of grace and truth. . . . From his fullness we have all received grace upon grace" (John 1:14, 16). As biblical scholar Gail O'Day writes, "God is made known in the enfleshed life of the Word of the world, and that life is one of fullness and grace." These verses "make abundantly clear, the incarnation is a moment of *fullness*. Flesh is where the action is—where the Word encounters and engages the world."[7] On emptiness: "Though he was in the form of God, he did not consider being equal with God something to exploit. But he *emptied himself* by taking the form of a slave and by becoming like human beings" (Phil 2:4-7a, italics added). The Greek word *kenosis* means to let go or to give of one's body/self.

We embrace fullness and emptiness in our body story as we learn to hold on and to let go. Examples abound for how we might do this: speaking truth to power, giving and receiving hugs, advocating for justice and peace, tutoring a child, opening the door for a person who is dis/abled. We decide how to live out our body story as we ponder these questions: How do we show up genuinely in the world and in our relationships? How do we actually serve others? A body story pays attention to what is actually happening and engages in real-life circumstances.

Our body story connects with Jesus's story and creation's rhythm. For Jewish and Christian people, keeping Sabbath is a religious command-

---

7. Gail O'Day, "Gospel of John," in *Women's Bible Commentary*, 3rd ed., ed. Carol A. Newsom, Sharon H. Ringe, and Jacqueline E. Lapsley (Louisville: Westminster John Knox, 2012), 519, italics added.

ment. The root of the Hebrew word for Sabbath—*shabbat*—means "to cease" or "to stop." We do well to keep in mind that not everyone has the luxury to stop. Some must keep going to generate income for food and shelter. Being able to stop and to rest becomes a justice issue that should concern people of faith and spiritual seekers across the globe. We advocate for systemic changes in organizations and public policy in order that all people might regularly have the opportunity to cease from labor and know restoration in their bodies: "And on the seventh day God rested from all the work that he had done. God blessed the seventh day and made it holy, because on it God rested from all the work of creation" (Gen 2:2b-3). *Sabbath observance is an affirmative practice that recognizes our bodies as sacred and nurtures our bodies' wholeness and capacity for relationship.*

In Sabbath, we reconnect with God's healing rhythm of creation. We can do this in other ways, too. We participate in this order in being awake and being asleep. Jesus himself is a model. When tired, he sleeps. It is the disciples who have a problem. They get upset and think they're being abandoned (see Mark 4:35-41). Jesus pays attention to his body. Sleep is a daily Sabbath, and ancient communities were better at it than we are. Researchers at the National Institutes of Health have observed when people turn off the use of artificial light from dusk to dawn, sleep cycles are enhanced. They describe a pattern in which people experienced "about four hours of deep sleep, woke for two hours of quiet rest, then slept for another four."[8] Between two sleep cycles, participants experienced a "state of consciousness" unlike any other they had ever known. We could think of these periods between sleep as "restful prayer or quiet meditation." Cutting off the use of artificial light is one practical way of allowing our body story to connect with God's healing rhythm. Sometimes, though, our bodies need artificial light to help us cope with mental health concerns such as a seasonal affective disorder.

> **Questions for Reflection:** Name one step you can take to "cease" throughout the course of a day, week, or month to create opportunities for mini-Sabbath? After you make the changes, what do you notice about your body's rhythm/story?

---

8. Clark Strand, "For True Sleep, Turn Off the Lights Earlier," *The Washington Post*, May 24, 2015, B5.

Chapter 1

Caregiving as Healing Practice

Caregiving is a healing practice of sharing power in relationship. Dr. Gawande is a world-famous physician who describes care approaches to help inform how we want to offer and to receive care. Our bodies ground us in the present moment and hold memories of the past. Gawande names two aspects of self-understanding: "experiencing self" and "remembering self."[9] Our "experiencing self" is what we encounter right now. It is direct and immediate reality. Our "remembering self" draws experience from the past that is being recalled in the present. Attention to our own bodies helps ground us and allows us to be available when another person shares a body story.

Gawande identifies three approaches: (1) paternalistic control approach: the caregiver acts as *a commander* by telling people what to do; (2) informative approach: the caregiver acts as *a technician* by providing facts and figures so people can make their own decisions; (3) interpretive or shared decision-making approach: the caregiver acts as *a counselor/coach* by providing information, helping people evaluate choices, and offering one's personal perspective.[10] I see pastoral and spiritual care as a counseling/coaching relationship: we help people make sense of and make choices through their body stories. We are neither commanders nor technicians, but we are caring companions.

> **Small Group Exercise:** Describe instances when caregivers acted as commanders or technicians of your story. What did you notice about your body's response? Now, describe instances of coaching and being companioned. What differences do you notice in the body's response?

Sometimes the "remembering self" and "experiencing self" converge in our bodies with unexpected force. Toni was a longtime member of a congregation. One Sunday she came up to me at coffee hour, and clearly she was visibly shaken. "Yesterday was an awful day for me." Her voice

---

9. Atul Gawande, *Being Mortal: Medicine and What Matters in the End* (New York: Holt, Henry & Company, 2014), 237.

10. Gawande, *Being Mortal*, 200.

dropped as she looked down. "Of course, it was even worse for the person who experienced it," she said. The previous day she had been out running errands when she witnessed an accident. A car and a motorcycle collided right ahead of her. The motorcyclist was thrown to the pavement, and she swerved to avoid hitting him. "I instantly thought of Paul," she said. "I've never seen a motorcycle accident before." Forty years earlier, her eldest son was killed when his motorcycle hit a tree to avoid an accident with a car. Toni never saw the scene, but the memory lives in her body. My words conveyed empathy with her body story: "It's like that day forty years ago happened yesterday." She wiped away tears.

Caring companions share reflection in the present as we help others wrestle with the past and the future.[11] We need to stay grounded in our bodies in order to be effective. The process is about discovery, not imposing expectations of what "should be." Volumes could be written on how various aspects of identity form and misform our body stories. What's important to remember is this: as caregivers, we listen for how a person's body story bears the wounds caused by stereotypes related to gender, age, race, sexual orientation, and many other aspects of identity. Our job as spiritual care companions is not to unpack all aspects of the identity box but to hear and believe the wounds are real. Listen and breathe intentionally to allow the other person's body to be. Each body story conveys aspects of similarity and difference with others in a cultural group.[12] Avoid clichés and trite statements that could shut down the body story. Notice the comfort and discomfort in your own body. Attend to unresolved dilemmas or unfinished business with your own body story.

> **Body Care Question:** What happens in your body when you recall or relay a difficult story? Notice changes in breathing, or placement of limbs, or heart rate, or tension in the stomach or back.

---

11. See Pamela Cooper-White, *Shared Wisdom: Use of the Self in Pastoral Care and Counseling* (Minneapolis: Fortress, 2004).

12. On this point, see R. Esteban Montilla and Ferney Medina, *Pastoral Care and Counseling with Latino/as* (Minneapolis: Augsburg Fortress, 2006), 11. The authors describe Latino/a people as belonging to a "multiethnic community" that includes many different cultures that together comprise a rich vibrancy.

> **Body Care Practices**
>
> **Photos as Mirrors**
>
> Photographs capture our bodies in time. When we glance through a photo album, we remember who we were "back then" and also see our bodies as if reflected in a mirror. We notice physical changes that have occurred and recall peak and valley life experiences. Gathering photographs creates a kaleidoscope of our body experience. Photographs tell a body story.
>
> **Body Care Exercise:** Choose one old photo and gaze at it for a few minutes. Ask yourself: What do I feel in my body now? What clues does it provide for my body experience then? What part(s) of my body story does this photo tell? What does it not tell?
>
> **Journal Reflection**
>
> Reading through old journals offers glimpses into our body stories. We might notice wrestling put to rest, impasses overcome, and old struggles in new form. The distance of time, hopefully, allows for an expanded and compassionate view. Not every journal entry, of course, tells a body story. But in our reading and reflection, we might stumble upon a few hidden or forgotten gems.
>
> **Body Care Exercise:** Select a journal from at least five years ago. Leaf through and note anything that strikes you about your body story: lack or abundance of exercise, eating patterns, emotional struggles, presence or absence of supportive family/friends. What changes, if any, do you recognize? What steps do you want to take to positively shape your body story?

Body as Storyteller

The body itself is a narrator, an "I" with a voice. Our bodies are storytellers with a specialized language. Body story is what's happening in the body at any given moment of experience. The story is not the chatter going on in our minds; it is, rather, more like a feeling or sensed reality in our actual bodies. The "I" or "ego story of the self" is our rational mind's generated commentary that may or may not be related to what is occurring in the body. Discovering we have a body story apart from the story of the self is eye-opening for some people. In spiritual care, we practice getting in touch with our own body stories and experience in order to help and guide others. People can sense whether we inhabit our bodies and selves in a relatively integrated whole. It is partially how others determine whether or not we are "genuine" or "authentic."

> **Care Practice:** Identify a situation of noticing your body story or that of another person. How was the body story connected or disconnected with the self-story?

Our job is to listen and to understand body stories. As Martin Buber artfully conveys, "The body does not use speech, yet it begets it."[13] To imagine the body—and more specifically our bodies—as conveyors of narrative requires a shift in viewpoint. We may see the body as an object of care but rarely as the subject, except when it is ill. We take the body for granted in deference to something more important that we call the soul. Body and soul belong together. We may only begin to pay attention when there is pain and suffering. We need not wait. We can learn to read body stories as a means to cultivate whole person care in the present.

Pastors and lay caregivers should never pretend to be physicians. We engage in spiritual care, not medical care. We sense, though, when Jesus says "heal yourself" that he is speaking about the whole of us, not soul and spirit. Perhaps we are rediscovering an old wisdom that has been lost along the way. Learning or relearning to hear, appreciate, and interpret body stories takes attention and patience. Our "body-selves" refers to "embodied being."[14] Instead of listening to stories *about* the body, we learn to listen *through* the body for meaning in stories.[15] We need to listen and think *with* the body.[16]

Listening and thinking *with* the body takes practice, and in time it becomes a form of "hospitality."[17] We learn to read and welcome body

---

13. As quoted in Arthur W. Frank, *The Wounded Storyteller: Body, Illness, and Ethics* (Chicago: University of Chicago Press, 2013), 2.

14. The term body-selves is borrowed from Kleinman, as referenced in Frank, *Wounded Storyteller*, 28.

15. Frank, *Wounded Storyteller*, 2.

16. Frank, *Wounded Storyteller*, 24.

17. See Emma J. Justes, *Hearing beyond the Words: How to Become a Listening Pastor* (Nashville: Abingdon Press, 2006), 1–20.

language as we gain familiarity with the practice. It's somewhat like developing facility with interpreting different kinds of signage on hiking trails in a national park. Guideposts on trails include a few signs with script, such as High Ridge Trail, 0.7 miles, with a directional arrow. Most trail markers, however, appear in a "natural" language: colors painted on trees or logs, stones piled at a switchback, or tree branches serving as roadblocks. It is vital hiker information. The body, too, conveys critical faith and life information if we pay attention, interpret the signs, and heed the markers: the body grieves, expresses joy, revels in delight, gets tired, knows hunger, and feels pain. Sometimes the body story message is clear and requires no interpretation. At other times, we take it one step at a time to sort things out.

We practice hospitality with body stories. Just as we would invite guests to our home and treat them with utmost respect and care, we can do the same for our bodies. Emma Justes suggests the practices of vulnerability, humility, thoughtful availability, and reciprocity.[18] We can apply these attitudes/practices toward our own and others' body stories. I have a friend who likes to make fun of her "organ recital," describing her body ailments and challenges. Not everyone is so cheerful with their body story, and for good reason. Some people are deeply weighted down by the stories their bodies are telling. It is hard to practice hospitality in such situations. But difficulty in listening to a body story does not mean we stop listening. Instead we develop *ways* to listen. Such a shift in attention can benefit us personally when we experience trouble. It can also be helpful in care with others. Through the stages of our body story, we can learn to adapt as necessary (not idolize youth, not denigrate old age, or shift in midlife). Gracious hosts receive guests just as they are.

Bodies tell stories that vary with life circumstances.[19] Many of us benignly neglect the body voice until problems occur, and then we can't ignore it any longer. Usually that time comes when we get ill. Arthur Frank outlines different types of stories people tell when ill. These nar-

---

18. See Justes, *Hearing Beyond the Words*, 7–17.
19. Frank, *Wounded Storyteller*, 18–19.

ratives are the way people "give voice to an experience that medicine cannot describe."[20] Spiritual care tends to body story and makes connections to God's good intention for life.

What are some of the stories the body tells? Frank categorizes the kinds of stories of illness that different "bodies" tell: the *restitution narrative* (*"I can get back to the health I had before."*): this story line assumes health is the natural state that can be restored; the *quest narrative* (*"I embrace things as they are and see life as an adventure."*): this story line accepts illness and makes meaning of suffering; the *chaos narrative* (*"I am completely overwhelmed by this and don't see a way through."*): this story line conveys being pulled into the unpredictability, disorder, and unraveling of life. People most fear the chaos narrative because it suggests disorder and disintegration that is often hard to fit into our mental worldview.

Some of us engage the *disciplined body*—we control our bodies by following prescribed regimens and directions; we become "super charged" to do everything right to make our bodies right. We whip our bodies into shape. Others engage the *mirroring body*—we try to create our bodies in the image of others whom we want to copy. Some of us engage the *dominating body*—we seek to take our frustrations and limitations out on others. We lash out at others when our bodies fail. Some of us engage the *communicative body*—we accept and take steps to live as fully as possible given new challenges and opportunities.[21] Body stories do not fit into neat categories. Caregivers help people give voice to whatever they experience. Through honest truth telling and listening, we navigate through the thicket of shame and open the pathway to God's healing grace.

We are not perfect but rather are "wounded storytellers." "What story do you wish to tell of yourself? How will you shape your illness, and yourself, in the stories you tell?"[22] Illness and life events mark our bodies in

---

20. Frank, *Wounded Storyteller*, 18.
21. See Frank, *Wounded Storyteller*, 40–52, 115–36.
22. Frank, *Wounded Storyteller*, 204.

Chapter 1

profounds ways. Dombkowski Hopkins discusses Nicholas Wolterstorff's lament over the death of his twenty-five-year-old son in a mountain-climbing accident. Wolterstorff speaks of the survival level of suffering "that demands our empathy and solidarity" and references the story of doubting Thomas: " 'Put your hand into my wounds,' said the risen Jesus to Thomas, 'and you will know who I am.' The wounds of Christ are his identity. They tell us who he is. He did not lose them. . . . In my living, my son's dying will not be the last word. But as I rise up, I bear the wounds of his death. My rising does not remove them. They mark me."[23] Life events and illness shape our body story in ways we cannot know in advance. Through the valleys, peaks, and plains of life, we remember God has created us as beloved body beings. We are called to live faithfully with/in our bodies as storytellers and story listeners. We are likewise called to justice by advocating and working to dismantle patterns and systems that silence and oppress body stories.

Each body comes with gift and choice. A pastor colleague once said: "Up until forty, we get the body we're born with. After forty, we get the body we deserve." The comment serves as an invitation and not as an indictment. Each of us is gifted in body, and we have some choice in how we live out our stories. We must also work to ensure that others have the freedom to live into fullness of their God-inspired story. For Christian churches and caregivers, chaos also needs to find a voice: "As part of our canon, psalms of lament offer us ready-made vehicles for the expression of chaos."[24] Laments provide language to keep talking with God at our most fragile and vulnerable times. There is no shame in that.

> **Questions for Reflection:** What story is your body saying about you right now? What shifts or adjustments do you want to make to sit in the driver's seat of your own body?

---

23. Denise Dombkowski Hopkins, *Journey through the Psalms*, rev. and expanded ed.(St. Louis: Chalice, 2002), 118. Dombkowski Hopkins quotes from Nicholas Wolterstorff, *Lament for a Son* (Grand Rapids: Eerdmans, 1987), 98.

24. Denise Dombkowski Hopkins and Michael S. Koppel, *Grounded in the Living Word: The Old Testament and Pastoral Care Practices* (Grand Rapids: Eerdmans, 2010), 140.

Body Care Prayer

Creator God,
You create and love our bodies.
Teach us to create and love as you do.
Show us the way in faith
To listen to
To hold on to
To let you go into
The story you live through us.
Amen.

Chapter 2

BECOMING BODY CONSCIOUS

A friend commented on stars depicted on social media wearing new outfits and stilettos to showcase their figures every day during the global pandemic when most people were sequestered at home in our sweats and slippers. It was a jarring disconnect to observe. We wonder: How do we absorb bodies' messages that leave us feeling as if, somehow, we don't measure up?

"You look good!" an older parishioner commented to a man several decades younger after not seeing one another in person for more than a year and a half. "Look at me, I'm so old!" Listening to interactions like this one may make us conscious of how we compare our bodies with others.

Body consciousness has come to mean something rather superficial in our culture. Instead of looking out for the well-being of others and ourselves, we lift up appearance and internalize self-judgment while leaving out what matters: genuine acceptance. It is easy to see how we get sidetracked: we are biologically wired to focus outside ourselves to guard against threats.[1] But when we look outside ourselves, we also take in harmful cultural messages (read: advertising) that relentlessly push us

---

1. Bessel van der Kolk describes how the "most important job of the brain is to ensure survival, even under the most miserable conditions. . . . The brain is built from the bottom up" with the "evolutionary older" parts devoted to "moment-by-moment management of our body's physiology and the identification of comfort, safety, threat, hunger, fatigue, desire, longing, excitement, pleasure, and pain." In Bessel van der Kolk, *The Body Keeps the Score: Brain, Mind, and Body in the Healing of Trauma* (New York: Penguin, 2014), 55–64.

toward imitating others instead of being ourselves. It's like we're fashioning another body to inhabit, just like a hermit crab![2]

In this chapter, we focus on becoming body conscious as a spiritual practice, which benefits us as individuals and communities, too. We benefit from letting go of the notion that body consciousness is sinful. In fact, body unconsciousness leads us to ignore signs and look the other way. When we lack consciousness, it's as if we sleepwalk through our lives. We leave ourselves open to being defined by and internalizing advertising and harmful cultural messages. God values our bodies. They are gifts for living out God's divine image in the world.

The Image of God and the Body

The book of Genesis provides the basis for what it means to be created in God's image. Humans are created on day six. The pattern for this day is different than the other days of creation; it is longer, and God speaks more than the narrator.[3] "Only humans are made in the image of God (Gen 1:26), and only they are given dominion (Gen 1:26-28)."[4] Dominion does not mean to plunder or dominate; it means to take care of. To be created in God's image imbues us responsibility for relationship. "The royal use of 'image' in the Ancient Near East is democratized here. All human beings, male and female, and not just kings, 'mirror God to the world.'"[5] In caring for our bodies, we reflect God's image. God needs our bodies to fulfill God's vision of the world. If we are busy copying others or trying to keep up appearances to fit in or please, we aren't doing our part to make the vision into reality.

Jesus is a model for being in his body and for our becoming body conscious. Mark's Gospel portrays Jesus as a person with very human reactions: he gets annoyed with the disciples (9:19; 8:17f); groans and sighs

---

2. I credit this metaphor to my colleague and friend, Denise Dombkowski Hopkins.

3. Denise Dombkowski Hopkins and Michael S. Koppel, *Grounded in the Living Word: The Old Testament and Pastoral Care Practices* (Grand Rapids: Eerdmans, 2010), 32.

4. Dombkowski Hopkins and Koppel, *Grounded in the Living Word*, 33.

5. Dombkowski Hopkins and Koppel, *Grounded in the Living Word*, 33.

(8:12); welcomes children for who they are, not as objects of teaching (9:36; 10:16); is full of compassion (1:41); loves the rich young man with mutual agape love (10:21); needs a cushion in the boat to sleep on (4:38).[6] Jesus is conscious of himself as a body person and lives out his call with this awareness. "Here is a Jesus who has a body, and the author of the Gospel of Mark has no problems about that."[7] Jesus is a spiritual teacher who is also deeply body conscious.

Jesus embraces his body and likewise connects with others' body concerns and needs. This is good news for people on a spiritual path of love and awakening. There is no shame in being bodies. What is shameful are all the culturally conditioned thoughts and practices that make people, and thus bodies, think of themselves as "less than," "not good enough," or "inferior." It is "a failed wholeness."[8] Becoming body conscious helps gradually peel away layers of conditioned shame.[9] We embrace the goodness of our bodies. We welcome our wholeness and let go of negative shame-based messages.

Shaming the Body

Do we say to our bodies and ourselves, "Shame on you for feeling that way!" "Shame on you for being that way!" Emotions can be tricky to work with because they seem to have a mind of their own. We can sometimes beat ourselves up for emotions that send valuable body signals. We tell ourselves: I am not supposed to be like this or feel like this. There must be something wrong here. This is especially the case for working with anger. "The capacity for anger is deeply imbedded in our brain and neurological system, and

---

6. See Elisabeth Moltmann-Wendel, *I Am My Body: A Theology of Embodiment* (New York: Continuum, 1995), 47.

7. Moltmann-Wendel, *I Am My Body*, 47.

8. Dombkowski Hopkins and Koppel, *Grounded in the Living Word*, 41.

9. Shame has both positive and negative functions that we learn about in relationship with others. Positive shame helps us to learn boundaries between self and other and to know and follow rules. Negative or conditioned shame has made us feel inferior and insignificant. For a theological resource on connections among wounding and shame and sin, see Andrew Sung Park, *From Hurt to Healing: A Theology of the Wounded* (Nashville: Abingdon Press, 2004).

anger is activated when something in life threatens us."[10] God created our brains and bodies with this capacity. We, of course, need to take steps to get to the source of the threat and determine its validity. But that we experience the emotion of anger does not in itself suggest anything is wrong with us. It suggests something is going right, if we can discern the source of the threat.

We may have spent years in therapy and pursuing spiritual practice and still find ourselves being challenged with emotions. The ability to work with emotions may shift depending on the context. We might do fine when relating with friends and companions with whom we feel comfortable. But when we encounter difficult situations in contexts that are either unfamiliar or unfriendly, we feel less equipped. Becoming body conscious allows us to come from a place of self-love instead of self-shame.

We cultivate healthy body consciousness by watching ourselves and letting go of negative shame-based practices toward emotions. These tendencies may be so ingrained and bound up with other cultural and spiritual messages that we may not realize how we are relating with emotional selves. Consider how you engage in and can let go of:

- belittling ("It's not that big a deal.");
- analyzing ("It must be related to an incident in my childhood.");
- facing down ("I'll stuff it and move on.");
- lecturing yourself ("If you would only learn to speak up."); and
- drowning in the feeling ("I feel really awful that I can't stop myself.").[11]

"Let my people go," Moses implored the Pharaoh of Egypt. Like the Pharaoh, we can hold our bodies and emotions hostage. We can also set them free.

Engage emotion-freeing practices with the body:

Say "yes" to our bodies.

Notice and resist negative cultural messages about our bodies.

---

10. Andrew D. Lester, *Anger: Discovering Your Spiritual Ally* (Louisville: Westminster John Knox, 2007), 29.

11. Eugene T. Gendlin, *Focusing* (New York: Bantam Books, 1981), 42–43.

Create connections with people who practice healthy relationships with their bodies.

Acknowledge bodies; do not render others "invisible."

Instill children, youth, and young adults with positive body messages.

Becoming body conscious is not selfish or self-centered. It is, actually, just the opposite. In an interconnected world, any step we take toward wholeness has positive effects for ourselves and others. An image from Buddhist and Hindu cosmology captures this reality. "Indra's Net" pictures every aspect of creation as an intricately interconnected net. At each intersection in the net is a jewel that reflects every other jewel.[12] Any change or shift to one part reverberates throughout the net. Beauty is reflected and refracted endlessly in the jewels. Imagine a spider's web shimmering with water drops. Envision a web with crystals sparkling with color. The image casts a purpose for the practice of becoming body conscious. We come to see ourselves not in a narrow, self-centered way but as part of an expansive vision and reality in which all bodies reflect divine image. We become body conscious in order to mend the net of God's creation by caring for *all* bodies.

> **Body Practices**
>
> Self-centered statements and practices come in a variety of forms. Notice what happens in your body when you: see people text mindlessly and talk loudly on phones; overhear a person talk about "being old" when he is much younger than others; endure someone complaining about "being taken advantage of" when they have significant economic means.
>
> Now, observe your body response when you listen to an elderly neighbor share his joy of sitting on the patio to "take in the greenery" when he used to sit inside; see a one-year-old take his first steps; learn of a friend needing surgery for a back injury; interact with a community member who is flourishing in his forties after a sudden cardiac arrest in his late thirties precipitated by a congenital heart defect.

---

12. For a useful resource on this image, see Rajiv Malhotra, *Indra's Net* (San Francisco: HarperCollins, 2016).

We recognize we're on a path of growth and awareness as we yearn to devote more time to reflective body practices. Even though we may get discouraged and feel impatient once in a while, we can own the experience and move through it with the support of others.

> **Question for Reflection and Discussion:** We practice using language to describe the body. Otherwise, it seems as if we are talking about something else. Name one aspect of your own body or others' bodies you are becoming conscious of this week. Ponder what people have told you and what you have observed. Share your reflections.
>
> **Practice:** This is an exercise in becoming conscious. How are you discouraged and/or impatient in your life right now? Can you own it? Rest in your own truth. Rest in your own integrity. Receive the truth and integrity of others.

Always Advent

In the Christian calendar, Advent (meaning "arrival" in Latin) is the four-week period before Christmas. Christians prepare for the birth of Jesus by reading scripture, lighting candles, and reciting prayers. We prepare in spirit and body through the central practice of waiting. Our bodies wait. We marvel at and wonder about new birth every day, an advent for the body's welcoming a new arrival. "Implying forward" is a concept used in focusing practice to signal "something that is alive is always in process . . . something alive is already preparing for its next step in its very tissues."[13] God is being born in and through our bodies every day. Sit for a couple of minutes. Ask yourself how you can open yourself to God being born in you today?

The Advent spiritual rhythm is preparation for new life, but we may notice thoughts about death also creep in. A pastoral counseling client said she grew weary of going to church during Advent because, in her words, "everything is too positive and upbeat. I always think about death

---

13. Ann Weiser Cornell, *Focusing in Clinical Practice: The Essence of Change* (New York: W. W. Norton, 2013), 15.

at this time of year." She didn't feel comfortable sharing this with many people. We may feel unable to voice similar thoughts.

As days become shorter and nights longer in the Northern Hemisphere, it is no wonder thoughts turn to death in this season of holy birth. Our bodies are attuned to the rhythm of God's creation. Birth and death are part of the cycle of faith and life. John the Baptist cries out in the desert, *Make a way for our God*. We make a way in advent by preparing for new life and welcoming—or at least not pushing away—thoughts of death. The practice is helpful for those who may be feeling low, lost, or lonely, which includes everyone at some point. Jane used to put up a Christmas tree every year, even after a divorce and her children left home. She dreaded doing it but thought her kids would be disappointed if she didn't. After agonizing for a while, she simply decided one year not to buy and put up a tree. She felt a rush of energy. While sadness still lingered, Jane made a way through Advent by discovering newfound delight in placing memorable objects and colorful garland around her home. By owning the death of what no longer was, Jane noticed her body felt relieved.

> **Question:** How might this Advent practice carry over into other times of the year?

Those who grieve during the season of Advent are heightened to the emotional experience of loss. Some churches offer Blue Christmas services especially for those who grieve. Such services give people permission to be with the weighty emotions of disappointment, grief, loss, and sadness. "Happy faces" are not required. We become body conscious as we honor in ourselves the complexity of life. If we are care leaders, we temper messages of peace, hope, and joy with validation of the season's experiential underside. All of us can create ritual space for welcoming birth and honoring death. Over time, we realize we develop positive body memory not by pushing the negative away, but by welcoming it as much as we can. This does not mean we want or desire the experience, only that we make space for and do not fight it. Death is part of Advent, not just Lent. Our bodies know this reality and call us to pay attention. In place of hope, joy, peace, and love, we might experience wonderful sadness, joyful grief, and hopeful loneliness.

> **Questions for Reflection:** What language suggestions do you have for worship that aligns with your experience and/or that of your community during Advent?
>
> What of the Holy is asking to be born in you or your community? How can you begin to create space, an embodied practice, for this new reality?

Observation of Body Connection

> **Story of a Little Boy**
>
> I overheard a child happily inform his grandmother, "I'm now 4 feet 3½ inches tall!" "Is that with or without shoes?" she asked. "Without," he answered. For most of us when we are young, we notice our growth. Over time, we become more aware of our limitations. Does it need to be this way? How might we choose, instead, to notice growth in all stages of our life?

Maybe like the little body, we develop in body consciousness by noticing and stepping our way toward change. Margaret Kornfeld identifies two kinds of change: "first order" and "second order" change. With "first order change," we "learn to function better," but our "basic situation" remains the same.[14] We might learn coping skills and strategies for interacting with an unreasonable boss or for living with an alcoholic spouse who misses family functions or for assuming responsibility on a work project to keep things on course. We change to fit the situation or system. However, when we come to see, believe, and act differently, then we notice a more radical shift. That is second order change at work. We no longer are willing to accommodate to the situation. Second order change takes immense courage. We may change jobs, leave an alcoholic spouse, or move to a new place after the death of a loved one. This all takes body consciousness. Our bodies tell us we need something different. Most of us inch our way

---

14. Margaret Kornfeld, *Cultivating Wholeness: A Guide to Care and Counseling in Faith Communities* (New York: Continuum, 2001), 7.

toward transformation. We might be willing to live with first order accommodation until we are ready for second order transformation.

Relaxed Observation

God moves in and through body experience to lure us toward transformational change. We get in touch with God and ourselves through relaxing into attention. Here *relaxed* means easeful being of body without grasping. We know ourselves not merely thinking about but also sinking into relationship with God.

Martin Buber uses "I-It" and "I-You" to distinguish between these two modes of consciousness.[15] I-You is direct encounter. I-It is an abstraction or idea, or indirect reflection. Imagine God as River. I-It relationship is like standing on the riverbank, watching the water flow, or saying, "That's a beautiful river." There is certainly nothing wrong with this mode of consciousness. We spend much of our lives in this state. We need ideas and abstractions to communicate with one another and to talk about God. Buber identifies another kind of relationship as "I-You" that can be experienced "only with one's whole being."[16] This mode has intensity to it. It is like standing or playing in the river. We might frame "I-You" as a living encounter with God that draws on the whole of who we are in body, mind, and spirit. It is not an indirect relationship of just thinking or talking about God, even though language is also an aspect of the "I-You" mode. As we become body conscious, we long to encounter God and share in relationship with the whole of ourselves.

"I-You" consciousness describes the experiential reality of what eastern spiritual tradition calls non-duality or "no separation" between subject and object.[17] We often live unaware of being connected with the whole of creation. We are part of it all. God, too, is not separate but is intimately connected with every aspect of creation. All is one. We experience unity or

---

15. See Martin Buber, *I and Thou*, trans. Walter Kaufman (New York: Touchstone, 1996), 53.

16. Buber, *I and Thou*, 62.

17. See Ruben L. F. Habito, *Living Zen, Loving God* (Somerville, MA: Wisdom Publications, 1995), 79; Cynthia Bourgeault, *The Heart of Centering Prayer: Nondual Christianity in Theory and Practice* (Boston: Shambhala, 2016).

oneness and call it a "God moment." Such experiences catch us off guard in a dramatic rush of energy, move us toward quiet connection, take our breath away, stir our hearts, or move us to tears. These moments are life-transforming and fleeting, and they affect our bodies. Body consciousness makes us available to the moments, but body consciousness does not create them. Consider Moses before the burning bush in Exodus 3:1-12. He stands on holy ground sensing the power to follow God's call. As Buber says: "You encounters me by grace—it cannot be found by seeking.... The You encounters me. But I enter into direct relationship to it.... All actual life is encounter.... The relation to the You is unmediated."[18]

I-You moments inspire awe. A parishioner shared his sheer joy of swimming outside as the sun set against a cerulean-painted sky. A silver moon shimmered through the barren branches of a nearby tree. It was truly a religious experience. The sense of seeing and being part of God's creation was simultaneously palpable and inexpressible. We encounter the holy in and through our bodies and often have no words to describe it.

> **Genuine Encounters in Care**
>
> I-You relationship with God energizes our bodies for care relationships. We come to value people for who they are and not what they can do for us or the community.
>
> We choose to say, "We haven't seen you at church in a while," which carries a tone of judgment. Instead we say, "It's good to see you." Pastoral and spiritual caring puts people first.

Our bodies are part of the mysterious wonder of life and experience directly what our words grope to express. Fortunately, we can turn to poets and poetry as a vehicle to capture this vital sense of aliveness encountered through our bodies. Poet Mary Oliver calls us to embrace ourselves within the beauty and order of creation. We do not need to earn a place through effort or merit. We allow ourselves to love our bodies, ourselves, as we are: "You do not have to be good.... You only have to let the soft animal of your body love what it loves."[19] The words convey gentle permission

---

18. Buber, *I and Thou*, 62.

19. Mary Oliver, "Wild Geese," in *Dream Work* (New York: Atlantic Monthly, 1986), 14.

to embrace who we are. Psalm 139:13-15 (NRSV) declares: "For it was you who formed my inward parts; you knit me together in my mother's womb. I praise you, for I am fearfully and wonderfully made. Wonderful are your works; that I know very well. My frame was not hidden from you, when I was being made in secret, intricately woven in the depths of the earth." God creates and knows us intimately. Coming to this realization and truly embracing this knowledge is an embodied I-You moment. It may prompt appreciative reflection and resounding praise.

> **Individual or Group Reflection Exercises:** Locate Mary Oliver's poem "Wild Geese." Read and reflect by yourself or in a group. How do the poet's evocative images give you permission to love your body and embrace your life? Read Psalm 139. How do the rich body metaphors shape your view of who you are? How does it feel to embrace being "fearfully and wonderfully made"?

I-You Moments

Fly fishing in the Idaho River
Sitting atop a mountain after a long hike
Being baptized
Receiving Communion
Praying
Gardening
Walking in the woods

> **Question:** What I-You moments can you name in your own life? How can your daily life be structured to make you available to I-You experience?

Gentle Observation

Body consciousness draws on our refined ability to experience and to watch. Theorists in several fields engage in "participant observation," a method in which researchers study people and cultural patterns.[20] We

---

20. For further description of this method, see Mary Clark Moschella, *Ethnography as a Pastoral Practice: An Introduction* (Cleveland: Pilgrim, 2008), 70–72.

become participant observers of our own bodies. Participant observation calls us to watch, listen, respect, notice, inquire, follow, and draw connections. We can adapt it as a frame of reference for body conscious care. Everything we encounter inwardly and outwardly can become an opportunity for "soft eyes" curiosity.[21] "Soft eyes" refers to a meditation practice of gazing at a point of reference and simultaneously allowing our range of awareness to expand. Just as an ethnographic researcher steps into an environment as learner, rather than as expert, so we, too, can harness the power of becoming participant observers of our body experience.

Here are participant observation tools adapted to learning about the body. Some of the tools we can use by ourselves, and some require conversation with others:

- informal interviews—Checking in with open-ended questions: how are things going?

- direct observation—Watching and feeling the breath and heartbeat, core body functions.

- participation in the life of the group—Noticing how you feel and react in different kinds of settings. What needs to be changed or enhanced?

- collective discussions—Sharing ideas and perspectives with trusted others around topics related to the body.

- document analysis—Keeping records such as exercise logs, eating records, or dream journals to become conscious of habits and patterns.

- self-reflection—Giving yourself space and time to consider what's good for your body.

- life histories and information gathered from online and other

---

21. This prayer/meditation technique involves keeping the eyes open and looking slightly downward. It can also be described as a reflective gaze.

activities—Reading widely and being open to new ideas and practices for growing in body consciousness as a person of faith.[22]

As body ethnographers, we practice what Clifford Geertz called a "thick description" of our subjective matter.[23] A thick description goes beyond the superficial and surface meaning to listen and explore in greater depth. We make use of various methods depending on the circumstance or situation. As body ethnographers and researchers, we may at times need to create a bit of respectful distance in order to gain perspective on a particular message. At other times, we may immerse ourselves in attending to multiple and perhaps conflicting messages only to find that threads of connection suddenly come together into a coherent story. We pay attention to everything—patterns and small details—not with a tight grip but with a "holding loosely."[24] We do not discount anything as we watch and learn. Pieces of the puzzle come together in time.

We seem to be natural participant observers in peaceful times such as sitting on the back porch or next to the riverbank. We notice what is happening "on the outside" and are quietly attentive what is happening "on the inside." We experience ourselves as simultaneously "part of" and "watching." We especially need the practice when we feel emotionally reactive, irritated, trapped, and frustrated. Instead of getting absorbed in our heads, we can stop to investigate what our bodies know.

> **Practice:** Try the role of becoming a participant observer. At various times during the day, take notice of your body when you are by yourself. What postures do you take? What feelings surface? See yourself in relation with others. What do you observe?

---

22. For a detailed exploration of ethnographic practices as a form of listening, see Moschella, *Ethnography as a Pastoral Practice*.

23. Moschella, *Ethnography as a Pastoral Practice*, 197–98. See Clifford Geertz, *The Interpretation of Cultures* (New York: Basic Books, 1973), 1–30.

24. See Donald A. Capps, *Living Stories: Pastoral Counseling in Congregational Context* (Minneapolis: Fortress, 1998), 205–7, 214.

Chapter 2

Body Consciousness and Care

Margaret, a pastoral counseling client, worked through being overlooked for a position at work, and she also wanted a relationship. "I sometimes feel like I'm being ignored," she said at one point. She then described a recent social interaction: "I walked up to a colleague at a social gathering recently and said hello. He glanced blankly and then proceeded to send a text message. Perplexed, she stepped away and noticed feeling agitated. Then, something clicked for her. She recalled our conversation about participant observing, "being in the moment," and "seeing there is not a thread directly between people." At first Margaret found herself spinning with her own thoughts about being ignored. Then, she stopped and noticed. Instead of fuming about how rude people can be, Margaret saw herself in a matrix of interactions. "It was not about me! They were just not paying attention," she exclaimed.

The body practice of participant observation expands the range of what we can learn and how we can care. We see what is "about us" and what is "not about us." It's as if we observe from God's eye view. Really seeing what's going on with us and around us is a freeing practice that has positive benefits at home, work, and in the community. Try it for yourself.

In caregiving, we need to observe and trust body messages. We don't want to jump to premature conclusions, but neither do we want to ignore information that presents itself. We note it and tuck it away for reference. A pastoral counselor relates a story about a child in a family who becomes physically sick about the time his father began having a secret affair.[25] Clearly there was an imbalance in the family system, and the child's body sent the message. Hidden information in the father's life manifests in a child's sickness, a sign of being triangulated between the father and the affair. The child's body reveals the secret.

A seminarian tells how her body held the hostility and tension in her parents' marriage. She writes: "I never really saw my mom deal with her emotions or anxiety except for working a lot. I would hear my parents ar-

---

25. Larry Kent Graham, *Care of Persons, Care of Worlds: A Psychosystems Approach to Pastoral Care and Counseling* (Nashville: Abingdon Press, 1992), 74.

guing very loudly. *It would make me so nervous I would start laughing and I couldn't stop.* It was the weirdest thing."[26] Bodies reveal unconscious material that may or may not directly belong to us. It is helpful to pay attention to our own body and work through any emotions that get hooked in us.

Staying body conscious allows care providers to be adept and present in caring for people. We notice physical symptoms and refer as necessary. We recognize somatization, which is the development of physical symptoms in relation to emotional distress. Spiritual caregivers work with teams of other professionals to help ease the pain people experience by listening to their stories and helping them take steps toward a positive future.

Spiritual caregivers need to do their body work throughout the phases of care. A colleague expresses her frustration with trying to help people who, in her words, "just wanted to talk" about their problems and "not do anything" about them. These clients, she suspected, did not want to engage as participant observers in their lives. They were observers and not participants. She would make suggestions and people would not follow up. They were like "talking heads" discussing issues disconnected from their own bodily experience. The therapist cares for her own body by practicing and teaching Pilates.

Our bodies signal change and transformation, and other people can help us notice the clues. Pastor Susan knew of Michele's apprehensions of online dating. She wanted to support Michele and not be intrusive. Pastor Susan embodied being a caring presence to help Michele become a participant observer in her relationships. "What are you most afraid of?" Pastor Susan asked. "Getting close" and "giving up" were the only words Michele could muster. "Okay," Susan said, "embrace your body messages." Michele eventually shared her experience of going out with Alex, with whom she enjoyed good conversations. "It's moving slowly," Michele offered. "But I noticed the glimmer in your eye," Pastor Susan reflected. Pastor Susan's mirroring of Michele's body message provided Michele a valuable source of reflection for her body consciousness. Pastor Susan helped Michele stay with her unfolding experience. Time would tell whether this was the *right*

---

26. Italics added for emphasis.

person. But already she knew the *rightness of staying with the experience* of meeting new people.

Dreams

Dreams provide clues to how we can become a participant observer with our bodies. John, a young professional in his late twenties, had completed a graduate degree in social work. He worked in an organization with entrenched dynamics. I saw him through a few months of pastoral counseling. One night he had a dream. While he thought it was relatively insignificant, he shared it anyway. "A frog appeared on a rock in the middle of this pond." He didn't know what to make of it, and he could not get the image out of his mind. "Be the frog," I said, drawing on my knowledge of Gestalt therapy. "What would the frog do?" I asked. "Leap!" he blurted out.

We can engage participant observation with our dreams. Here are questions to prompt consideration of dreams from the body's perspective: How and where is the body positioned in the dream? How does the body shift and change? What is the body's relationship with other things or people in the dream? What is the body doing? What kind of human or animal body is portrayed in the dream? What does its nature and habits suggest for your life?[27]

Mission Statements

Churches and spiritual communities are well-served by including the word *body* in mission and vision statements if the desire is to grow in consciousness and serve the world. The precise language needs to reflect central theological commitments since mission statements are touchstones to guide community practice. Sometimes, the word *body* appears explicitly in a statement (such as "we embody the good news").[28] Sometimes, *body* is implied (such as "we seek to live out" or "to be beacons of light").[29]

---

27. We can practice dream interpretation alone or with a group. Consider this resource: Kelly Bulkeley, *Big Dreams: The Science of Dreaming and the Origins of Religion* (Oxford: Oxford University Press, 2016).

28. See Christ Congregational UCC, Silver Spring, MD, www.cccsilverspring.org.

29. See Davis Community Church, Presbyterian Church (U.S.A.), Davis, CA, www.dccpres.org.

The statements focus a community's energy. Some churches already have intentional health care ministries, so the explicit statement may simply lift up a community's good work. Wellness checkups, blood pressure screenings, workshops on end-of-life care, and educational forums on matters of suffering and thriving for bodies of all ages are valuable for members and the community. Communities can also include the body in their guiding statements even in the absence of financial resources for robust programming. Doing so signals the body's integral relationship to God and to the practice of our faith.

Statements serve as outward commitments and inward reminders of how we live the image of God in the world. They need to appear in prominent public places. A congregation in Washington, DC, developed a new statement of mission, included it in the weekly worship bulletin, and recited it every Sunday for one year and then monthly thereafter. Individuals can also develop mission statements and then follow them. Growth in body consciousness needs this kind of intentional practice.

> **Questions for Reflection:** How could you revise your mission statement to be more explicit regarding consciousness and care with the body? If you were to write a personal mission statement, what would you say and how would you share it with others?

Body Care Prayer

God of Life,
You create us as blessed, embodied beings and help us grow from unconscious to conscious life. Let us not squander our lives in frivolous pursuit of empty self-images and instead see our purpose in your image. Open our hearts with gratitude to engage as hospitable participants in our lives and communities. Companion us as we wake to wonder and call us forth in peace. Inspire us to embrace ourselves and one another in loving care. Amen.

Chapter 3

STAYING WITH OUR BODIES

"When your body is rebelling, it forces you to pay attention," Lydia commented about receiving a cancer diagnosis on a Tuesday and being admitted for surgery the next Thursday. A whirlwind of thoughts and emotions swept through her in the span of a few weeks, from first symptoms to the stage of recovery. "I was worried about you," her friend Jane told her. Lydia sighed, "I know, and I felt bad that it affected you and others." We cannot help but be affected by what others are going through. It is a sign of care as we bear one another's burdens.

Staying with our bodies can be especially hard work during times of change and transition. Some of us, like Lydia, do not seem to have a choice. Illness forces us to take notice. Those of us inclined to care for others are unaccustomed to giving ourselves attention. It feels as if a glaring spotlight is pointed right at us. We shift and squirm and would rather flee and hide. But instead, we notice this uncomfortable sense, however slight or intense it may be, and learn to stay with our bodies. Each step we can take in this direction allows us to tune into our body story and its call toward wholeness. As we shift our attention in this way, we might notice ourselves becoming more aware and sensitive to other bodies, those of other people, animals, and creation itself. We open our hearts to the beauty and fragility of life and come to see our faithful work as embracing the world itself as God's body.[1]

God's Body and Our Bodies

Staying with our bodies may sound like a strange thing to do. After all, it does not really seem like a choice since we are embodied beings. "Staying with our bodies" is a way of naming a host of practices that includes intentional inward attention. Staying practices tune us in to our own and others' needs for care. In fact, our bodies are a science project in action. You might wonder: How is my body connected with others? Simply realize all bodies need air in order to breathe and have life. The air does not belong to anybody; all bodies depend on it.

Our bodies teach through direct experience about the interrelationship of everything in creation. Theologian Rosemary Radford Ruether calls for "[reshaping] our relation to our own bodies, to other embodied humans we have inferiorized as indentured labour and finally to the earth itself" as a "key to a sustainable future."[2] The distress and disease of our bodies can be symptoms of larger system imbalances and injustices. We might easily become overwhelmed at the magnitude of global problems. We participate in a hope-filled future in caring for the world as God's body as we take up a piece of the work and build connections with others around us. Staying connected with our bodies—or becoming reacquainted if we are alienated from them—grounds us in the ability *to feel* what is needed in our environment and surroundings. Psychiatrist Alisa Moreland-Capuia puts it this way in her work for justice on behalf of youth: "The 'feeling space' is the birthplace for genuine sustained change."[3] She draws connections between brain development and cultural awareness to offer practical methods for care. Knowledge informs our ability as individuals within systems to respond with justice-informed care that honors the integrity

---

1. See Sallie McFague, *The Body of God: An Ecological Theology* (Minneapolis: Fortress, 1992).

2. Rosemary Radford Ruether, "Re-evaluating the Body in Eco-Feminism," in *The Body and Religion*, ed. R. Ammicht Quinn and Elsa Tamez (London: SCM, 2002), 48.

3. Alisha Moreland-Capuia, *Training for Change: Transforming Systems to be Trauma-Informed, Culturally Responsive, and Neuroscientifically Focused* (London: Springer Nature, 2019).

of all bodies. Caring for our own and others' bodies as part of God's body entails tuning in and rebalancing systems for the well-being of all.

Practices of staying put us in intimate touch with God. In her model of theology, Sally McFague envisions the world as God's body. This imaginative framework calls us to practices of care in our lives *right now*, not in a distant future. We get involved with whatever is calling attention to us, like getting in our garden. We see the need for pulling weeds, fertilizing ailing plants, and pruning overgrown bushes. Knowing *about* the garden and getting out *in* the garden are different metaphorical ways to relate with God. We love God by caring for God's body, the world. Everything in the garden reflects the Divine whose power is expressed in the ability to make gardens grow. McFague calls this God's "ever-flowing sharing," of which we can get a sense of life-cycle power when we stand in a garden; we marvel and mourn at the growth and death. We see directly (life growing and dying or what Christianity calls God's immanence) and indirectly (the mystery that "makes it happen" or what Christianity calls God's transcendence). The image of God as Gardener and each one of us as tenders of this garden helps us see the interrelationship between caring and creation.

> **Creatures in the Garden**
>
> A gardener's sensibility helps outside the garden. While riding his bicycle along a familiar route, John happened upon a turtle stopped in the middle of the road. Unsure what to do, he stopped and watched. A woman driving by got out of her car and said, "This won't work." She meant: waiting for the turtle to move is futile. She then picked the turtle up and placed it near a grassy creek bank.

As body selves we are part of the garden wherever we go. Not every encounter is as benign as watching a turtle in the middle of the road. At times, we come face to face with threatening forms of life such as snakes, wasps, and bears. Staying present with our bodies requires steadfast focus as we make rapid decisions about anxieties and fears provoked by our encounters with other bodies.

Chapter 3

Imagining the world as God's body helps us see ourselves and everything else in creation as integral to an ongoing, organic process. This vision stands in stark contrast to a mechanical view[4] that sees the world as a machine with various parts with the smallest serving the largest. Parts are seen as fixable and replaceable. Interrelationship suggests mutual influence: for example, plants draw nutrients from soil, which can in turn be nourished by the plants that serve to hold the ground in place. Mechanical parts do not interact in this way.

A mechanistic worldview, in short, envisions God as separate and above creation, having started it in motion but now only intervening when God desires. This image of creation casts the Creator as the Grand Puppeteer of a passive world. A machine model values "the abstract, the universal, and the disembodied." This model is the template into which all life needs "to fit." An organic model, conversely, sees the common creation story (the consensus model of the Big Bang) that embraces "unity" as a complex, dynamic movement: "unity of nothing" that began an "irreversible historical process" and includes a unity of "unbelievably diverse bits of matter."[5]

> **Questions for Body Care and Spiritual Reflection:** How do you sometimes treat your body like a machine? How and when have you been captivated by animals or plants in God's garden? What did you experience in your body?
>
> What difference does it make to imagine God's body and your own body as a garden that needs tender care? What practices are called for?

Perhaps we cannot fully grasp what it feels like to stay with our bodies. So let's approach the question from the other side. How do we leave or escape from our bodies? Here, again, body experience needs to be the guide since we do not all take leave in the same way. Still, a few familiar escape patterns include practices commonly referred to as addictions that may temporarily make the brain and body feel good but have longer-lasting negative effects. They include using chemical substances such as drugs and alcohol, overeating, gambling, and engaging with multiple sexual partners.

---

4. McFague, *Body of God*, 5.
5. McFague, *Body of God*, 45.

Making Our Home in the Body

The opening of the movie *Patch Adams* conveys a spiritual lesson: "All of life is a coming home."[6] Our bodies can be friends and guides in the process. We chart our life path and navigate all life transitions with our bodies. We wonder: can we "be at home" in the transition we are making right now? Can we make friends with our bodies as a way to work with anxiety so that whatever we are moving through does not overwhelm us? If we are graduating, getting married, changing jobs, moving to a new location, or deciding to retire, we are in transition. It can be exciting and scary at the same time. Navigating different kinds of transitions is the work of a lifetime. As young adults, we leave home, and if we have been fortunate enough to experience an environment where people loved and cared for us, then we journey into the unknown with an internal sense of security. If not, we must care intentionally for ourselves and reach out to others in order to construct a secure enough sense of body and self for being in the world. Being home and leaving home represents a paradox, seemingly contradictory experience, which "is expressed in different ways throughout our lives."[7]

Here is another paradox: we are not fully defined by our bodies, and yet we are nothing without our bodies. We do well to pay attention to their signals and cues. At times the body can be "stubborn," like a dog pulling back on a chain or hugging the ground in protest. The body can be "boundless," like a dog freely chasing birds at the beach. Life transitions may not be easy even when we are looking forward to them, and it is important to give our bodies their say. The body holds paradox too: its experience carries a mixture of emotions that leaves us more like a dog turning in circles for just the right place to sleep. Each new life possibility, regardless of its adventuresome lure, also brings the undertow of grief and loss. A friend was surprised by a body response at her own wedding. Standing in the doorway, ready to walk out, she realized she had to sit

---

6. Tom Shadyac, Director, *Patch Adams* (Universal Pictures, 1998).

7. Herbert Anderson and Kenneth R. Mitchell, *Leaving Home* (Louisville: Westminster John Knox, 1993), 26.

down. Tears started to flow. "I just sat there and cried, then I stood up, and we got married." The practice here is "stopping, welling up, and walking through." A graduate student realized after deciding to switch degree programs that her body *felt at rest*. This was body confirmation of making the right decision. Being at home in our bodies opens us to take the next faithful step.[8] We cannot know what that is until we know it in the moment, and our bodies provide useful clues.

Anxious Bodies

A colleague once described anxiety as "stepping on the gas and the brake at the same time." We simultaneously push ahead and stop. Making our way through transitions can feel like that, too. We may want to push the gas pedal to go through faster, or the brake to slow our approach. Either way, anxiety reigns and it feels "yucky." Systems theory suggests we do not get rid of anxiety and fear. We instead develop habits of body and mind that help manage anxiety so we can be at home with ourselves and others. Sometimes anxiety and fear manifest in our bodies as agitation or irritability, lower-grade versions of the emotions. Sometimes we find ourselves taking it out on others. We need to get to the source of the dilemma to refrain from wreaking havoc in our bodies and on our relationships. It could be that we are trapped in a triangulated relationship between two people or things. A triangle is formed when two (people) pull in a third to stabilize what feels uncomfortable. Triangles serve a couple of purposes: (1) to absorb anxiety and (2) to cover over basic differences and conflicts in a system.[9] Our bodies pay the price in triangles. Imagine being torn between sympathizing with your boss and a coworker who are at odds, or between your spouse and a child over an important family matter. A couple of practices help manage the anxiety and in turn care for our bodies: (1) reposition or de-triangulate by giving

---

8. My colleague at Wesley Seminary has written a book on effective leadership that urges pastors and congregations not to take on too much, but to "take the next step." See Lovett H. Weems, *Take the Next Step: Leading Lasting Change in the Church* (Nashville: Abingdon Press, 2003).

9. Ronald W. Richardson, *Creating a Healthier Church* (Minneapolis: Augsburg Fortress, 1996), 116.

the emotional work back to those with whom it belongs[10] and (2) engage self-differentiation by clarifying your purpose and role; it is a matter of being an "I" and not overtaken by the "we." Our bodies will thank us.

We can stay in relationship with ourselves and others when every fiber in the body wants to fly or run. Let's look to the Psalms, a rich theological resource that teaches us "different kinds of prayer and many different ways of praying to God that articulate the entire range of human emotions."[11] The Psalms give us language to express where and how we really are. They "engage our whole person" on the journey to wholeness.[12] Consider Psalm 55:4-8 (NRSV): "My heart is in anguish within me, the terrors of death have fallen upon me. Fear and trembling come upon me, and horror overwhelms me. And I say, 'O that I had wings like a dove! I would fly away and be at rest; truly I would flee far away; I would lodge in the wilderness; I would hurry to find a shelter for myself from the raging wind and tempest." Clearly the psalmist wants to escape as a body storm rages. She would rather be anywhere else but where she is. It is a tension-filled place. "Stop this! I want to get out of here." The psalmist steps on the brake and the pedal, and the body holds it all. The psalmist gives us a clue and presents us with a conundrum in verses 12-14 (NRSV): "It is not enemies who taunt me—I could bear that; it is not adversaries who deal insolently with me—I could hide from them. But it is you, my equal, my companion, my familiar friend, with whom I kept pleasant company; we walked in the house of God with the throng." The psalmist simultaneously wants to crawl out of her own skin and stay in it. Her body is equal, companion, friend. It is a part of her she wants to escape, but she cannot.

This turns things "outside in." We want to flee from others—from those who humiliate, shame, belittle, mock, and in general make us feel small, insignificant, and vulnerable. *We want to flee our bodies because of what we do to ourselves or because of what others do to our bodies.* But "others" can never do this without permission; we control our internal responses, even though it seems as if "others" are doing this to "us." Being able to see

---

10. Richardson, *Creating a Healthier Church*, 122.

11. Denise Dombkowski Hopkins, *Journey Through the Psalms*, rev. and expanded ed. (St. Louis: Chalice, 2002), 1.

12. Dombkowski Hopkins, *Journey Through the Psalms*, 14.

what gets hooked in our minds and how it manifests in the body allows us to stay with it—to create a space for it to be there. God, too, has a desire to flee. In Jeremiah 9:1-2: "If only my head were a spring of water, and my eyes a fountain of tears, I would weep day and night for the wounds of my people. If only I could flee for shelter in the desert, to leave my people and forget them—for they are all adulterers and a bunch of crooks." Even for God, keeping the covenant promise takes an emotional toll. God wants to flee relationship with this wayward people. What does it require for God to stay? God has to tolerate in God's "body" the frustration of staying in relationship with the people. God is affected. God stays in relationship and works internally with the costs. We can do this as well.

Body Compassion

Staying present begins with love and compassion for ourselves. Imagine relating to one's self as an infant or little child. We generally speak attentively and kindly, with a sense of caring or a softer tone of voice. We ask with curiosity: "What's the matter?" Infants, of course, have no language facility so we must instead listen and observe. Imagine relating with such compassionate curiosity toward others' and one's own body: "how is it with you" is the question we ask quietly to ourselves, and then we listen and observe. The response might come in jagged form with fits and starts, just as a child might speak through heaves and sighs and tears. We hold ourselves and others at such times: "to hold" means "to be present with and to allow for what needs to happen." This is how we embody compassion. We do not say "figure it out" and "move on," which are harsh words that alienate us from ourselves and each other. Staying present opens curiosity and kindness in the mind as it settles anxiety and fear in the body.

We tune in to know what to do. "Staying with ourselves through body experience" does not mean we force ourselves to stay in any particular situation or environment. Actually, it is just the contrary. In truly listening with the body and staying with ourselves, we recognize that either can be a faithful response depending on the situation. It is a matter of discernment that involves the whole of ourselves with God's help. The word *discernment* comes from the Greek *diakrisis*, which means "knowing through hardship or difficulty."[13] We engage this practice when we encounter a bump or fork in the road.

Arlene hit a bump and left her mainline church congregation. She went in search of supportive practices for cultivating body compassion and tried out bikram yoga. She did not like being told to bear increasing levels of pain. Arlene knew intuitively this did not feel right, heeded her body's wisdom, and said no to the practice. Through a circuitous route, she came to a striking insight about her faith: God is not about punishing people "for their own good." Her journey to include the body intentionally in faith allowed her to embrace a new image of God: Lover of the Body. "Life has enough pain. God does not add to it," she concluded. Arlene returned to her local congregation when she discovered it was offering small-group Bible studies that included compassionate body practices.

Practicing compassion with the body and life experience was not the focus in the early years of the clinical education movement for pastors and church leaders.[14] Confrontation methods in group process were, instead, at the forefront. It was a "break them down in order to build them up" mind-set that I find problematic since it skates so closely to abuse. If we believe "this is painful so it must be good for me" thinking, then we have an internalized belief about God and ourselves that needs examination. Learning may be uncomfortable at times, but it should not leave us feeling worse about ourselves. If a person or group follows the "break them down" method, we need to assess our need to leave. In pastoral and spiritual care relationships, we should only trust people when they demonstrate their ability to be trusted. Consider this litmus test question: with this person or in this environment, do I feel at home in my body?

---

13. For a useful resource on discernment, see Elizabeth Liebert, *The Soul of Discernment: A Spiritual Practice for Communities and Institutions* (Louisville: Westminster John Knox, 2015).

14. To learn more about the history of clinical pastoral education, see Charles E. Hall, *Head and Heart: The Story of the Clinical Pastoral Education Movement* (Atlanta: Journal of Pastoral Care Publications, 1992). Current clinical education sites can be located at www.acpe.edu.

Chapter 3

Not Punishing

We mistakenly believe that punishing our bodies brings order to chaos. We might go through a "if only" list of ways that we blame ourselves and thereby gain a sense of control: if only I would have taken charge earlier, if only I had noticed the names left off the list, or if only I had planned more carefully. The list goes on. A colleague remarked, "I kicked myself for making that mistake!" That's punishing language that compounds the pain. We might be good at escalating the punishment as the importance and magnitude of the situation increase. The mind game leaves us stressed and distressed and bereft of energy for making a positive difference going forward. It is a helpful practice to own our part in situations and work through emotions such as grief, sadness, and regret. But we need to drop the punishing language. If we are more inclined to punish or blame others, we need to stop and take a closer look at that. **Question:** What do we hope to accomplish with punishing ourselves?

We also "punish" by trying to fix a situation or person instead of staying with our bodies through the discomfort and suffering we encounter. We may fear coming close to the pain or struggle of another person, so we jump into a "fix it" or "here's what you need to do" mode. If we find ourselves giving knee-jerk advice, then we're certainly in the realm of fixing. It may feel as if we're being helpful, but we're not. Perhaps we're not the one doing the fixing but the one being fixed. That certainly does not feel good, but if we are clued in enough, we can use the occasion to learn how not to relate with others. Regardless of whether we are the ones offering or receiving the advice, we know that some form of "punishing as pushing away" internal body experience is going on. It is a defensive form of body protection and self-protection. A helpful image to depict body presence in helping people through life transitions involves neither punishing nor pushing away but instead features accompaniment as with a midwife or another person. Midwives accompany a process.[15] As women and men who seek to help, we accompany others and ourselves through the natural rhythms of life. We learn to take our cues from our bodies.

---

15. For an expansion on this image, see Karen R. Hanson, "The Midwife," in *Images of Pastoral Care: Classic Readings*, ed. Robert C. Dyktra (St. Louis: Chalice Press, 2005), 200–208.

The biblical prophets were like social midwives. They accompanied God's people, helping them through the ups and downs of keeping covenant. They soothed the people in times of distress and warned people in times of impending doom. Prophets were not removed from the experience of the people. They very much felt and absorbed it. The prophets model being in touch with the body as a way to know God and people. The prophets know God as a real, pulsating reality, not as an abstract idea. As Abraham Joshua Heschel reminds us, prophets were "overwhelmed by the grandeur of divine presence."[16] They listened to God with their whole bodies and from this receptive space they speak words of true speech.[17]

Being present with suffering is how we care for people in transition. The way to the other side is through the pain, and not around it. In this journey, we listen. We listen as people sometimes punish themselves for what is happening, even when that punishment seems like nonsense to us. Why the punishment? It is a way to gain control; to impose a structure or meaning feels like more solid ground. Otherwise, we feel like we are floating at sea. The biblical prophets suffer as they stand in the "in-between" place between God and the people.[18] It is not an easy place to stand. Hear the soul cry from Jeremiah 8:18-19: "No healing, only grief; my heart is broken. Listen to the weeping of my people all across the land: 'Isn't the LORD in Zion? Is her king no longer there?'" As readers, we wonder if it is God or Jeremiah speaking in anticipation of suffering to come. Jeremiah feels the pain of broken covenant promises in his body. Ezekiel is told not to mourn the loss of his wife (24:15-16), just like the people living in exile could not mourn. As caregivers, we need to know how our bodies are affected as we minister with people in times of transition. It is helpful to become increasingly comfortable with the body experience of being unsettled, which is what transitions often bring up.

---

16. Abraham Joshua Heschel, *The Prophets* (New York: Harper & Row, 1962), 16.

17. Michael S. Koppel, "The Prophets and Pastoral Care," in *The Oxford Handbook of the Prophets*, ed. Carolyn J. Sharp (Oxford: Oxford University Press, 2016), 615.

18. Koppel, "The Prophets and Pastoral Care," 611.

Chapter 3

Owning the Anger

Prophets sit with people through pain in times of transition. They also call the community to account for breaking God's promises. The prophetic texts of the Old Testament do not speak to individuals but to a whole group. In practices of care with individuals, then, we need to pay special attention to the rhetorical dynamics of prophetic messages. We exercise care so individuals do not heap blame and punishment on themselves for that which the community needs to take responsibility. We speak up and do not practice passive silence in such situations. Misuse of the Bible and harmful theology take a toll on the body. We learn to stay present with our bodies and practice care in order to build resilience and foster resistance.

This is especially true in working with the anger that comes in times of transition. Andy Lester names anger as "the physical, mental, and emotional readiness to attack whatever threatens our survival."[19] God created us wired for survival, and our brains signal when it may be in jeopardy. "[W]e do not feel anger unless our brain interprets something in our situation as a threat."[20] Threats can be physical. Threats can also be psychological, or that which we interpret as under attack such as our beliefs, values, sense of right/wrong, social order, and so forth.

Transitions can open us to unexpected threats, leaving us feeling angry and not knowing what to do with the energy. Turned outward, anger can be destructive as it causes fights and spoils relationships; and anger turned inward on ourselves fuels resentment and despair. In order to harness the creative potential in anger, we can take several steps: (1) recognizing anger; (2) acknowledging anger; (3) calming our bodies; (4) understanding why we are threatened; (5) evaluating the validity of the threat; and (6) communicating anger appropriately.[21] Dealing directly with the anger opens opportunity to make new choices.

---

19. Andrew D. Lester, *Anger: Discovering Your Spiritual Ally* (Louisville: Westminster John Knox, 2007), 13.
20. Lester, *Anger*, 14.
21. Lester, *Anger*, 61–85.

> **Question for Reflection:** Call to mind a recent experience with anger, and consider the steps outlined above. What difference do you notice in your body as you get in touch with a threat?

Soothed in Silence and Wonder

We may rather flee than deal directly with threats and bothersome experience. That's okay, too. In a tension-filled, inward space, imaginary or real fleeing can, paradoxically, carve out new dimensions for staying. Regardless of whether we take actual steps to leave or just imagine possibilities, we still can reap physical benefits. Staying in a place not of our initial choosing as long as our physical safety is not in doubt can open into sacrament, a vehicle for revealing God's grace and spirit. Leaving or fleeing is exactly what the prophet Elijah does in 1 Kings 19 when he fears for his life. Elijah has killed "all the prophets," and now his own life is in jeopardy. The first time Elijah goes into the wilderness, he does so because he is driven by fear and despair. Emotionally distraught, he has to be encouraged to eat and to drink. Twice God asks Elijah what he is doing (v. 9 and v. 13); God's questions provide Elijah an opportunity to express his frustrations. God hears Elijah. The second time, God sends and accompanies Elijah into the wilderness. "Hang in there. We're in this together," God communicates to Elijah. Perhaps the realization settles into his body that he can do this. He can face the fear and anxiety that has left him distraught and grasping. He does not give up, but instead he finally gives himself over to facing the inescapable Presence that enlivens him for a new dimension of call. Clarity dawns and new possibilities emerge for Elijah as he encounters God in the "sheer silence" (1 Kgs 19:12 NRSV). When he is ready to stay present in his body with no external enticements to distract, Elijah knows in his bones and feels in his gut that he is called to be a blessing and to bless others. Elijah is soothed in silence.

An attempt to flee always seems to have a boomerang effect. We, too, run in order not to face what needs to be faced. But the opportunities keep showing up until we stay with ourselves at a fundamental level and know that God is with us as we do this deep work. No one can do it for us.

Wilderness and Wonder

The wilderness strips us down to the essentials. We begin to see the mind loops that keep our bodies spinning in circles. Consider how we engage in:

Rationalizing: talking ourselves into or out of a course of action or decision as a means to quell an anxious or fearful sense in the body

Comparing: making ourselves feel larger or smaller (inflating or deflating self-esteem) through contrast with our "ideal best" from another stage in our own lives or with other people

Fantasizing: fueling a story line that cannot be realized in this lifetime

Resisting: pushing away what already exists in some form

Letting go of the mind loops helps us to stay grounded in our body experience right here. This is the place from which authentic action emerges.

Staying in Our Bodies

Notice what keeps calling for attention. What is the thing you might put off or push away but still has a tug or pull to it?

Drop old habits. What habits or rituals distract you or whittle away your attention?

Welcome the "haunting voices," the internalized negative messages that sap vital energy. Surrounding them with sheer silence dissipates their power.

Embrace resistances. In time, we make space and build toward genuine welcome for that which may be initially fearful and anxiety producing. We discover a newfound freedom.

> **Practices for Staying in the Body**
>
> **Checking in Practice:** Can we check in with our bodies by carefully asking: "What are you running from? What do you need to say?"
>
> **Not Fleeing Practice:** Healthy-minded and spiritually alive people want to grow and to learn and face challenges that open unrealized vistas of possibility. Life may not always present contexts and situations in which this happens. Perhaps we feel stuck where we are.
>
> We might name this body experience as "treading water," "going through the motions," "in a ditch," or "in a rut." Life energy feels blocked or pent up. It might be in the predictability of a job or the comfort and boredom that comes with a long-term marriage or relationship. How do we generate motion when we are stuck but do not want to flee? Pay particular attention to agitation, frustration, impatience, boredom, and restlessness. How do they manifest in the body? What need is being covered over? What would it take to get things moving again?

Rest a While

Jesus says to the disciples who had been busy in ministry with him: "Come by yourselves to a secluded place and rest for a while" (Mark 6:31b). These words ironically enough can be difficult to embody for those occupied with many tasks. We may have become habituated to the mode of "too much to do with too little time to do it." Resting for a while is permission simply "to be," released from the need to do one more task right now. This is more than just "good advice"; it is gospel for the body. Rest allows for the germination of creativity and imagination. We can see ourselves, others, and the world with "new eyes" when we are rested. Without rest, we become drained and depleted. We become edgy and irritable.

Jesus knows the disciples need stillness and time to recharge in order to avoid "care and compassion fatigue." He calls the disciples to retreat for a time, away from pressing demands, so they can reconnect with themselves, to know themselves as blessed and whole. Amidst the call to rest comes this observation from the Gospel writer: "When Jesus arrived and saw a large crowd, he had compassion on them because they were like sheep without a shepherd" (Mark 6:34). The word for *compassion* is *splanchnizomai*, which means "churning of the gut." Jesus has a visceral body response to the people's physical and spiritual needs. The Hebrew word for *compassion* is *rechimin*, which means "womb love." Compassion is not just a thought or a feeling; it is known in and through our bodies. His compassion is a "gut response" that prompts care for people. He reaches out to provide for body needs: real food (the "miracle" of the loaves and fishes results in everyone having something to eat) and spiritual needs (teaching and healing).

Jesus knows something about staying with the body that modern people need to relearn. "Resting a while" is not just good advice; it is liberation for the body. Resting is restorative and key to being creative.[22] Unfortunately, not everyone has the luxury to engage in rest. Some people have to work multiple and wearying jobs just to make ends meet. We need not wander as "sheep without a shepherd." It seems a pitiful way to live. Instead, we can claim the body-restorative message Jesus delivers: you are complete. You are already whole. Know this from the inside out. Hear my words. Do not keep wandering and searching for others to tell you. Know it in your gut as I love you through mine.

> **Touch and Go Practice**
>
> It's a challenge to be in the present. We would rather retreat to the past or run toward the future. Through this desire to dislocate ourselves from current reality, our bodies pay a heavy price with illness, stress, and tension. Meditation teacher Pema Chodron suggests a practice for coming back to the present moment. It takes work, but "the effort is very light."[23] The instruction of "touch and go" helps us stay with our bodies as companions for our faith journey.[24]

---

22. Mihaly Csikszentmihalyi argues that creative people need to allow for "mysterious time" in order to incubate creativity. See *Creativity: Flow and the Psychology of Discovery and Invention* (New York: HarperCollins, 1996), 98.

23. Pema Chodron, *The Places That Scare You: A Guide to Fearlessness in Difficult Times* (Boston: Shambhala, 2005), 30.

24. Chodron, *The Places That Scare You*, 30.

> **Practice:** We notice our thoughts and fantasies and lightly touch them. To "touch" is to notice the thoughts and fantasies as such, and let them go.
>
> **Notice the Difference in Your Body:** So often when we realize we're locked in our heads or spinning in circles, we get angry at ourselves and become aggressive. Instead of allowing a harsh internal voice to dominate, we can use a lighter touch and notice what happens. Imagine the process as "relaxing our struggle, like touching a bubble with a feather."[25]

Uniting Our Bodies

The word *yoga* comes from the Sanskrit root *yuj*, which means "to unite, marry, yoke, or turn two into one."[26] Individual awareness unites with universal presence.[27] In the Hindu tradition, throughout its history, there have been many forms of yoga, including meditation, ritual ceremonies, austere physical postures, and breathing practices.[28] Postural yoga, or the *asanas* most people encounter in gyms, schools, and spiritual communities, is a modern adaptation.[29] Many people across the globe practice yoga, and often they do so for physical appearance and enhancement. Yoga practice can be helpfully adopted by Christians and other spiritual seekers as a vehicle for staying rooted in our bodies. We seek to unite our bodies and purpose with God's body and purpose in the world.

My first teacher was a Roman Catholic woman who spent years in India. Sister Ishpriya urged the practice of yoga asanas (body postures) *before* sitting in silent prayer. The rationale is, if the body is stressed or tense, then it will be reflected in a "noisy" mind. The tension, stress, pain, or discomfort in the body becomes an obstacle rather than an avenue to

---

25. Chodron, *The Places That Scare You*, 30.

26. Liz Stillwaggon Swan, ed. *Yoga Philosophy for Everyone: Bending Mind and Body* (West Sussex, UK: Wiley-Blackwell, 2012), xi.

27. Swan, *Yoga Philosophy for Everyone*, xi.

28. Swan, *Yoga Philosophy for Everyone*, x.

29. For analysis on this topic, see Mark Singleton, *Yoga Body: The Origins of Modern Posture Practice* (New York: Oxford University Press, 2010).

Chapter 3

deeper realized connection with God, self, and others. Engaging the body clears our mind chatter and opens us to the experience of *being*.

Various resources including classes, videos, and books inform yoga practice. As a Christian, I draw on these educational materials and opportunities to support daily practice. Yoga realigns the body and orients attention to being with, and not just thinking about, God.

Yoga aligns body and mind to stay in the moment. Through practice, we learn to notice internal and external critical judgments and their effects on us. The inner critic or harsh judge always seems ready to evaluate negatively our difficulties and shortcomings. The voice starts with a stem like this: "Why can't you just . . . ?" "Why are you always so . . . ?" or "Can't you just drop it?"

> **Questions:** Do you recognize that even you have this critical voice?
> What does your internal critic usually say?

Yoga makes us increasingly attentive to this voice in ourselves and others. Through practice, we learn to stay with our body experience by (1) detecting the judgmental voice and hearing what it has to say; (2) noticing strong emotions that get elicited in our bodies; (3) opening into the body posture(s); and (4) continuing to breathe and release. Gradually as we let go of the critical voice, we sense the integrity of our own being. We are who we are and we are how we are. In this moment, we intuitively know ourselves to be in alignment with God's presence.

Difficult People and Situations

Staying with our bodies becomes a daily practice, and it is not an esoteric ritual reserved for private spaces. The following care scenario showcases the emotional and physical challenges of negotiating relationships in a work environment. This is a composite narrative based on the stories shared by a spiritual-direction client over the course of several months. Names and other relevant information have been changed to ensure confidentiality.

Sandra and Robert work on the same teaching team at their school. One considers team teaching a dream; the other considers it a nightmare. Sensitive, smart, and creative, Robert likes to draw energy from others and is highly motivated in his areas of expertise. Even though he wants to be part of a team, he exhibits an inability to let go of control in order to become a learner while others lead. Robert is an excellent teacher and meeting organizer and a creative curriculum developer. However, he easily gets offended when people do not take his suggestions, and he has a difficult time sitting on the sidelines. He elicits positive and negative responses from others. People get frustrated with being unable to connect with him since he does not always listen and is easily offended. Everyone else is "the problem" in Robert's book. Still, he is always trying to help and insists on doing things his way. People eventually tune him out and avoid him, except in situations when his viewpoints and grandstanding will benefit them.

Team teaching is not Sandra's thing. She likes to have control over her own work without having to spend extra time coordinating with others. She, too, is a creative and engaging teacher with rave reviews from students and community members. Sandra and Robert have different styles of relating with children (one of them prefers to coddle some children while disregarding others and cultivates favorites, while the other one sets clear rules and guidelines with consequences for everyone to follow). Some children respond more readily to each of the teachers. Clearly, different styles suit different kids. No one teacher can reach every student, no matter what. The same can be said of most helping professionals.

Sandra has no choice but to work in the team and wants to develop a collegial relationship. But she is beside herself. She has tried every way she can think of to get through to Robert: direct conversation, email, and friendly written notes. Nothing seems to work. "What should I do?" she pleads. For several conversations she simply seems to be venting her frustration. She wants it "to go away" instead of really working with and through the relationship. "How would staying in your body feel in this situation?" I ask. Initially Sandra responded with a quick answer, "I can't do that. This whole experience is driving me crazy." Then she let the question settle in. Instead of pushing the experience away, how would it be to welcome it in? Instead of pushing her anger and frustration aside, how might it be to stay with them in her body? Instead of projecting and stuffing her uncomfortable feelings and judgments, could she stay with the experiences "just as is" without needing to change or to fight them? Sandra pondered these questions and keenly sensed the need to stay with her body as a way through the difficult work relationship.

We, of course, want to know how the story ends. We perhaps hope an idyllic encounter of mutual understanding occurs, one that resolves the interpersonal tension and establishes a harmonious working relationship. Our preference for this story springs from a "fix it" mentality. We instead stay with the body story and let it show the way.

Work and Community

We might yearn for "being one with" people or having what Freud called the "oceanic feelings" of bodily and spiritual connection experienced in our mother's womb. It is fantasy, sure to dash our expectations. Spiritual communities hold out the promise of attaining religious bliss, and work environments promote collaborative team-building in which members carry their weight. However, high hopes are often not realized on the ground, as Robert's story illustrates. Embodied practices for staying with ourselves and negotiating real needs point the way forward. It is embodied rebalancing. I was once riding an escalator in Atlanta and noticed the steep incline and what people were doing to steady themselves: they instinctively leaned forward to balance against the sense of falling backward. We do something similar in order to get our needs met. We have needs for connection, physical well-being, honesty, play, peace, and autonomy.[30] Needs are essential to life. We may be unconsciously adjusting at work or in the community in order to get our needs met. Perhaps it is time for a body rebalance?

We rebalance our bodies by paying attention to met and unmet needs. If needs are not being met in one environment, we do well to see how to meet them in another. Sandra is not going to have her need for autonomy met while working with Robert. So, it is vital to locate another domain in her life where this need can be exercised. Otherwise, dissatisfaction lingers

---

30. Deborah van Deusen Hunsinger and Theresa F. Latini, *Transforming Church Conflict: Compassionate Leadership in Action* (Louisville: Westminster John Knox, 2013), 24.

in the body and casts a pall over other experiences. So, too, Robert has a deep need for affirmation that goes unmet in his personal life, so he seems to demand it to a greater degree at work. A supervisor could compassionately confront him about the work behavior since it puts so many people off balance.

Direct communication is usually best to make our needs known. However, it may not be prudent or wise to be direct since the environment or the people involved may not be open. Instead of pulling back or leaning too far inward, we stay with our bodies and meet our own needs. This, too, contributes to community.

Body Care Prayer

Ever Present One,
You alone are the Giver of Life and present with us in and through our lives. At times, we do not know how to be present with ourselves as circumstances pull and push us well beyond our comfort zones. We would rather crawl out of our skin than stay in it. We would rather flee or hide than be in this moment. We would rather forge ahead unaware of what occurs within us and around us. Your presence halts us and calls us back to ourselves and to you. Like Moses, we stand before the burning bush and are awed by your passionate flame burning before us and within us, and listen to your voice calling us to stand right here on this holy ground. Amen.

Chapter 4
FOCUSING AS HEALING PRACTICE

During a church retreat, a group of participants sat in a circle waiting a turn to practice a body-focused exercise. An elderly gentleman took a turn with the leader who guided participants to focus on their bodies and identify images to describe their experience. Over and over again, Ted responded to the questions with his head. He kept saying, "I think . . . ," instead of "I sense . . ." or "It seems like . . ." or "I feel . . ." Caught up in his head, he seemed unable to connect with his body. This was not entirely surprising. Ted was eighty-one years old, and after having endured knee and hip replacements that left him walking with a cane, his body was becoming more of an unwelcome guest than a friend. What his body did know was that it liked to take naps! Watching this tableau of interaction deeply affected Mark, another participant in the group. As Mark listened to Ted's fits and starts in his attempt to get in touch with his body experience, Mark felt the tears flow. Mark realized that he, like Ted, lived "in his head." The tears signaled a flowing release of something previously constricted.

> **Questions for Reflection:** Where and how in your life have you noticed a thawing or releasing? What made it possible? What changes followed?

Releasing may bring tears for some people as it did for Mark. Tears are a release of emotion. But as we will explore further, crying is not just getting in touch with our emotions. We are encountering the body's story. In fact, Mark was in imaginative dialogue with the workshop leader. As Mark heard the workshop leader engage Ted around his body experience,

Mark was asking the same thing of himself, "What is it like in your body?" The response he heard was: "It is like something is being wounded again and again." Mark's body felt heard. The flow of tears signaled a releasing of what his body had been holding. It felt like grief. But there was more. The tears came with a strong inner sense of a river flowing against a landscape of vivid color. This body metaphor reflected what Mark understood as God's new life rushing through him. Fear and hubris and plain old "not knowing how to connect" separate us from body knowledge.[1] Like the participants in the opening story, many of us need gentle guidance in turning toward the body as a source of wisdom.

This chapter explores embodied emotions and showcases practices for individuals and groups to tune in to our bodies. We listen to our bodies to know ourselves and to tap God's transforming process already at work within us. We know that change is the nature of life and cite the oft-repeated phrase, "The only constant in life is change." We know this in our heads but lose touch with our bodies. We tune in to our bodies to be available for the next life step already emerging.

Beginning Steps in Focusing

Success in counseling, according to psychologist Eugene Gendlin, comes when we tap into the immediacy and source of our body experience. "Your body 'knows' the whole of each of your situations—vastly more aspects of it than you think."[2] Getting in touch with the body's knowledge allows us to grope our way to clarity. A counselor or caregiver helps guide and witness the process of a care seeker moving into their own body experience. It's a process filled with fits and starts. Words and phrases do not come out of mouths in neatly formed statements. We try out a few words, a partial image, and a few seemingly disconnected impressions to get at what's going on. Here's the thing: such utterances indicate people being *in touch with* experience and *not simply talking about* it.

---

1. Bonnie Miller-McLemore argues that the "hubris of the modern mind sustains a certain disdain for our mammalian bodies and the knowledge gained through them." In "Embodied Knowing, Embodied Theology: What Happened to the Body?" *Pastoral Psychology* 62 (2013): 755.

2. Eugene T. Gendlin, *Focusing* (New York: Bantam Books, 1981), viii.

"Experiencing" describes the "directly felt here-and-now process . . . the inward sense where we find what we mean."[3] "Experiencing" is connecting with the "inner direct referent" or felt meaning in the body.[4] Felt body experience includes but is not limited to emotions and feelings. Neither is the body experience "merely physical or somatic."[5] "Gendlin redefined the 'body' as 'interactional living process.' The body is our 'lived experience.'"[6]

We can use whatever terms suit us to name a dynamic reality: "experiencing," "felt body sense," "inner direct referent," "felt sensing," and "body felt experience." Basically, the body carries intelligence on its own. When we are in touch with this intelligence, we live in closer connection with God, ourselves, and others.

> **How Emotions and Felt Senses Differ**
>
> Emotions are nameable and knowable; felt senses are hard to define.
>
> Emotions come in culturally expected places; felt senses are unique to the individual person's life situation.
>
> Emotions narrow our awareness; felt senses widen our awareness.[7]

Presence

The word *presence* captures the aim of spiritual practice and caring relationships. Presence means to show up in our bodies with mindfulness and heart. Ann Weiser Cornell uses the phrase "self-in-presence" to name how to be in relationship with our bodies. Some of us feel absent or scattered more often than we sense ourselves present. We long to find ways to be "one with ourselves," neither disconnected nor overly identified with feelings. A poster with three scenes captures how to move into

---

3. Ann Weiser Cornell, *Focusing in Clinical Practice: The Essence of Change* (New York: W. W. Norton, 2013), xviii.
4. Cornell, *Focusing in Clinical Practice*, xix.
5. Cornell, *Focusing in Clinical Practice*, 8.
6. Cornell, *Focusing in Clinical Practice*, 8.
7. Cornell, *Focusing in Clinical Practice*, 49.

a healthy, connected relationship with our feelings and inner experience.[8] The poster is called "The Three Guys." On one side is a man with a red cloud around his whole body, and the caption is "I am angry." This person cannot separate from emotions. The person is overly merged with feelings. The poster depicts another man with a red block behind his back, and the caption reads, "I am not angry." This person is dissociated from feelings. The third man has a red cloud around his belly labeled as "something" with an arrow pointing to "I," and the caption reads, "I'm sensing something in me is angry." This person is connected with body experience and feelings. The message is clear: a partnered relationship with our bodies is ideal. We neither merge with nor dissociate from feelings, but instead we create a bridge.

> **Practice: "Something Is Happening"**
>
> Let's practice with using the word *something* to name experience. Instead of reacting to a person or situation by becoming overwhelmed with feelings (merger) or separated from feelings (dissociation), stop and check in. You do not need to know what is going on in order to partner with it. Take a few deep breaths and say kindly to yourself: "Something is happening here." Let the inner experience show you what it is.

Body Language

Focusing is a means to get in touch with the change that is already underway in our bodies. We can practice alone or with others. It is not about changing ourselves, but getting in touch and listening. We may already have some tools necessary for this practice. It is not a matter of lots of new learning, but rather it is about using these skills of listening attention in a slightly different way. This point alone gives us the encouragement to give it a try. What's the difference? Consider the felt body experience as the "third" person in a conversation. So, for example, it is not just pastor and parishioner or therapist and client, but rather it is care provider/care seeker/felt body experience/sense. The focus is on the third one—the body experience in the moment. Think of the body experience as a full partner

---

8. Cornell, *Focusing in Clinical Practice*, xxxiii.

in the conversation. What happens when the body experience is shy or doesn't want to speak? Don't gang up on the body and force a response. Be patient. Treat the body experience as you would honor a treasured friend. Don't get pushy. Be respectful. Give space. Practice graciousness. The friend will speak in due time, if it wants. Don't over-focus on the body or felt sense. The goal is not to glare or stare but to observe and allow. For some people, even the use of the word *body* may be a stumbling block.[9] Find alternative language such as: what do you notice *here* (signaling the throat, chest, abdomen, or stomach).[10] Often felt senses show up in the middle area of the body, but they can emerge anywhere in the body.

Tend to the body, and use language with care. We never know when we might inadvertently encounter an emotional minefield in others or ourselves. A minefield is an unconscious body story that gets provoked. We don't know what experiences of trauma people may have had or if they hold negative or distorted images of their bodies.[11] The gentle practice of focusing can still be used, but exercise care to avoid emphasis on "body" language. Instead of asking, "How do you experience that in your body?" simply ask, "How is that for you?" or "How is it to be with *this*?" [implied is the felt sense or whatever is being experienced in the moment]. We might discover in using focusing as a spiritual care practice that a person needs referral to a psychotherapist or another trained professional. We might become aware of this need in ourselves. That's a good thing.

If we imagine felt senses or body experiences as our "client," we can bring an attitude of curiosity to hearing more about the story. This open perspective embodies a core teaching in the Christian tradition that encourages welcoming the stranger. Emma Justes offers four aspects of hospitality for relating with strangers: vulnerability, humility, thoughtful availability, and reciprocity.[12] Let's explore briefly the meaning of each component.

Vulnerability entails opening to risk on an emotional level. A felt sense may show us something that surprises us about ourselves and our

---

9. Cornell, *Focusing in Clinical Practice*, 73.

10. Ann Weiser Cornell, *The Power of Focusing: A Practical Guide to Emotional Self-Healing* (Oakland, CA: New Harbinger Publications, 1996), 29.

11. Cornell, *Focusing in Clinical Practice*, 73.

12. Emma J. Justes, *Hearing beyond the Words*, 7–16.

situation. Be open to surprise. Humility means approaching with right proportion and being grounded in an awareness of limitations. A felt sense probably teaches us something we do not know and need to learn about our current reality. Be open to learning. Thoughtful availability means to give space to hold and ponder. A felt sense asks that we pay attention to *it* in its fullness. Be open to receiving its offering. Reciprocity means listening, and care requires give and take. Just as a therapist helps a client, so does the client give something to the therapist, usually by way of satisfaction in offering beneficial help. The more we open ourselves to felt senses and learning from body experience, engaging in the process itself becomes a more natural part of our faith lives.

Listening is building a bridge of connection with felt senses and body experience. Just as a therapist would embody compassionate listening with a client, so, too, can we practice empathic listening toward our own and other people's felt senses. Better yet, we can imagine ourselves engaged in harmonious or interpathic listening.[13] *Interpathy* is a term used in intercultural care to describe a respectful attitude and accompanying skills for attending and responding that assumes differences rather than similarities. In Revelation 21:5, God says, "Look! I'm making all things new." God does not flip a switch and make it so. God moves in and through creation, including our bodies, to birth this new creation. Instead of approaching felt senses with an "I know" attitude, we assume an "I don't know" perspective. We assume the body is teaching us something we do not know or may have forgotten. With open-minded and open-hearted posture toward body experience, we welcome what is appearing within, even when it is strikingly different than we expect. We might be "hosts to angels," God's ambassadors, without knowing it (Heb 13:2).

Interpathic care is needed most especially when we are reactive to experiencing. When we are fearful or impatient with the felt sense, or when we try to figure it out or push it away, we can simply be with *that*.[14] "Treat each guest honorably," Rumi writes in his poem "The Guest House."[15] We

---

13. Denise Dombkowski Hopkins and Michael S. Koppel, *Grounded in the Living Word: The Old Testament and Pastoral Care Practices* (Grand Rapids: Eerdmans, 2010), 161–62.

14. Cornell, *Focusing in Clinical Practice*, xxxii.

15. Jalal al-Din Rumi, *The Essential Rumi*, trans. Coleman Barks (San Francisco: HarperOne, 1997), 109.

might rather not have a particular guest who has shown up (quivering and quiet sense in the stomach, aching and longing sense in the heart, or whatever it is). If we cannot welcome the guest, then we *recognize that we don't want to* welcome the guest. When we lessen resistance and stop reacting, we give permission for our experiencing to be just as it is.

Focusing as a body care practice allows each of us to move at our own pace. It draws on the body's natural intelligence that shows up in "implicit" felt experience. The "solution" to a dilemma presents itself as we turn inward to listen.

> **Strengthening the Bridge through Practice**
>
> Interpathic care with experiencing requires practice. When alone or in care conversation, we build the bridge with our body experience by inviting and nurturing felt senses and easing our inner resistance to whatever emerges. Practice for care: start the day by saying to yourself, "I will welcome whatever experiencing occurs." In care conversation with others, stay present and ask, "How is that for you right now?"

Groups and Focusing

Focusing on body experiencing can be introduced unobtrusively in group settings. We, of course, do not want to turn every group into a therapy session. Yet, professional leaders and caregivers recognize that if you do not care for people and what they care about, little constructive work will get done. Group lethargy or resistance sets in and old patterns repeat.[16] These same tendencies occur with individuals. It is not our role to intervene in care practices with individuals unless people initiate conversation. We have a general care responsibility to tend to the group or community as a whole. It is appropriate to introduce theory and practices that enhance living together into God's covenant community and fulfilling the community's mission. We might introduce a group to the practice of "simply noticing."[17] We can invite people to pay attention to their

---

16. Cornell, *Focusing in Clinical Practice*, xxxv.

17. "Notice it" is the phrase used during EMDR, a therapy for working through trauma; there is no need to make sense of or explain an experience; just notice it.

body experience in the group setting as a practice of listening to God. It is helpful not to look for quick results, but to let the process and people's participation in it (or not) lead the way. We open ourselves as individuals and as community to God's revealing work through us.

> **Experiencing in Group Settings**
>
> Make physical space hospitable. Create space for individual and corporate reflection that allows for body, heart, and head.
>
> Allow for people to share or not share as appropriate; this should never be forced, and people need to be given the chance to "opt out."
>
> Pace discussion for body awareness as appropriate.
>
> Pause and breathe deeply periodically.

An Everyday Spiritual Practice

In my spirituality and care course, the emphasis is on discovering and engaging practices that work for individuals and communities. Focusing with the body can be a practice that fits into our daily rhythm since it is not labor intensive. We just need to be willing to check-in with attention. Here's a list of suggested ways to guide your daily practice, beneficial for self-healing (Cornell) and connecting with God (my addition). Remember: it is not about following a prescription; try on what works for you and let go of the rest. Think of it as practice on the go. Once people internalize the process, it can be used in lots of places and in lots of ways.[18]

(1) "Which way today?" Pause for two minutes at the beginning of your day. Ask yourself: what, specifically, needs attention today? Or simply ask your body to show you what needs attention.

(2) Relax and pay attention inwardly to your body. Scan from your throat to your chest to your stomach to your abdomen. "Your body is like an empty stage waiting for the curtain to go up [for the play]."[19]

---

18. Adapted from Cornell, *Power of Focusing*, 25–32.
19. Cornell, *Power of Focusing*, 27.

(3) Rest attention in the middle of your body and ask, "What wants my awareness now?" or "How am I about that issue?" This is attuning with the body. Notice what comes up and find a few words to describe it if you can, such as "weighty sadness," "anxiety in the stomach." Be gentle and patient with yourself.

(4) Acknowledge what you sense by "saying hello." This is an important step of honoring and valuing what is real and true in your experience at the moment.

(5) Refine the name. Fill out the description you began to name above. Play with the language until it seems to "click" with the body. "Weighty sadness" in the chest might become "trying to hold something up and feeling really sad." A word, an image, a metaphor, or some combination might describe what you sense and allows the body to feel "heard." You sense resolution, relief, or release. Your experience might feel complete as it is, or you might now know the next steps you need to take.

(6) Check back with your body. Imagine speaking directly to your chest and saying, "Trying to hold something up and feeling really sad, is that right?" Notice the shift in your body as it feels heard.

Janet Abels, a teacher of focusing, describes the practice as putting the "head brain" in touch with the "body brain."[20] Throughout the day, we can connect our different "brains." It is one way to fulfill the Apostle Paul's admonition to pray without ceasing.

> **Daily Practice:** Develop a habit of consciously "checking in" with your body at least once a day. This brief "check-in" serves to reset mind-body alignment. We might "think" God has one thing in mind for our day, only to check in with the body and encounter a different sense of what is being called for.

---

20. Cited from an unpublished workshop information sheet.

Chapter 4

Getting in touch with and being able to express feelings is a first step toward healing.[21] For people accustomed to living in their heads, it is like entering a whole new world, which can be exhilarating and frightening. Healing, though, involves more than personal feelings and has a range of meanings that can be hard to pin down. For pastoral psychotherapist Margaret Kornfeld, healing is a mysterious process that is already underway as people reach out for help: "something has already moved within them that has allowed them to reach out and ask for help."[22] Caregivers and communities facilitate and complete the process as they reach back with supportive spiritual resources. For Old Testament scholar Walter Brueggemann, healing involves "restoration and rehabilitation of persons to their full power and vitality in the life of community."[23] We recognize the process of healing has reached a stage of health when people are "stable enough to share in the cost and joys, the blessings and burdens of the community."[24] Pastoral theologian Chanequa Walker-Barnes argues that the goal of healing for Black women, and I would add other marginalized persons and groups, is not to fit a burdensome idealized self-image. Healing involves "the journey of self-discovery and self-definition."[25] Together these definitions name healing as holistic health and well-being for individuals and communities. Body-awareness methods foster deepened self-understanding and help us grow in the ability to make genuine emotional and spiritual connections and contributions in community. The practices open a pathway for experiencing, knowing, and loving God. Our intention for starting a practice or seeking conversation with a care provider or other knowledgeable person often comes from a sense of "lack" or "dissatisfaction." Or perhaps we're stuck

---

21. Gendlin, *Focusing*, 9.

22. Margaret Kornfeld, *Cultivating Wholeness: A Guide to Care and Counseling in Faith Communities* (New York: Continuum, 2001), 74

23. Walter Brueggemann, *Living toward a Vision* (Philadelphia: United Church Press, 1976), 182.

24. Walter Brueggemann, *Living toward a Vision*, 181.

25. Chanequa Walker-Barnes, *Too Heavy a Yoke: Black Women and the Burden of Strength* (Eugene, OR: Cascade, 2014), 170.

in a "rut" and need help making an adjustment. Whatever it is, we can choose a path of healing and try what works for us.

Focusing is "the next step in development" after naming and claiming feelings.[26] This practice is the opposite of venting, a release valve for expressing (usually "negative") feelings. Venting feels good and serves a purpose in some contexts when we don't have control over making changes or decisions. Venting, though, is a closed loop. Focusing and other body-oriented healing practices expand awareness of our inner landscape. If we find ourselves venting or meet others who regularly vent, we might use the conversation as a springboard to go deeper. Invite people to break out of the loop. The body is longing for something more. Apostle Paul writes, "We know that the whole creation has been groaning in labor pains until now; and not only the creation, but we ourselves, who have the first fruits of the Spirit, groan inwardly while we wait for adoption, the redemption of our bodies" (Rom 8:22-23 NRSV). Focusing puts us in touch with the inward groan and God's healing restoration of our bodies.

> **Questions for Reflection:** Can you sense how you "groan inwardly" as part of God's creation?
>
> How are you experiencing "labor pains" in your own spiritual life?
>
> Can you identify steps for tapping a group felt sense (helpful for developing vision/mission statements and starting/renewing/ending ministry projects)?

Going Deeper

Let's explore how to go into our body experience. The steps and questions can be adjusted for our personal and community needs.[27]

---

26. Gendlin, *Focusing*, 9.
27. Gendlin, *Focusing*, 49–51; Cornell, *Focusing in Clinical Practices*, 21–22.

Fostering a supportive and trust-filled environment. Create and support a friendly, welcoming environment that invites trust. An environment in which we attack, criticize, dismiss, evaluate, or judge ourselves or others does not foster trust.

> *Practice Step 1:* Relax and direct awareness to your body. Scan the area from your throat to your abdomen. Now, ask yourself: "How am I?" or "How is my life going?"

Allowing for a "felt sense" in the body. A felt sense is a "freshly forming, wholistic sense of a situation that has a 'more than words can say' quality about it."[28] How do you know you are experiencing a felt sense? Signs include: is present in the here and now; actually occurs somewhere in our bodies; has a hard to name quality about it that calls for fresh, metaphorical language in order to describe (e.g., "kind of like a wall inside"); relates to life situations and contains more implicit information than what we have previously known.[29] We can *invite* a felt sense to form (intentionally making space to pause and look inward) and *nurture* it when it does (through being curious about, describing, and dialoguing with the felt sense).

> *Practice Step 2:* If many issues come to you after asking the questions in Step 1, ask yourself: which one feels most important right now? Allow yourself to be with what is primary and notice what occurs in your body.

Staying with the "felt sense" through direct experience. Imagine the felt sense as a visitor whom you would like to get to know. The purpose is not to "think" about the visitor but to be with it. The felt sense reveals more of itself when we welcome it. Ways to practice hospitable welcome include being with, staying with, and keeping company.[30]

> *Practice Step 3:* Welcome whatever comes up in your body experience. Acknowledge the presence of whatever you sense. Allow it to be there. See it as an entity separate and yet connected to you. Is there a word, image, or phrase that this sense suggests?

---

28. Cornell, *Focusing in Clinical Practice*, 42.
29. Cornell, *Focusing in Clinical Practice*, 43
30. Cornell, *Focusing in Clinical Practice*, 113.

Describing the felt sense. It is good to give yourself and others permission to grope toward finding just the right language that resonates with what is being experienced. Imaginative phrases, metaphors, and phrases such as "it seems like" or "it has the quality of" may be the best way to name the sense being experienced.

Practice Step 4: Stay with the felt sense in your body. See if a word, image, or phrase "fits" with it. Adjust the language until it seems to "click" with the sense. You may notice a shift or change in the felt experience.

Being compassionate presence in relation to the felt sense. The felt sense is our partner in becoming more aware and partnering with God in healing and growth. Practicing compassion toward our feeling, bodied selves may not come easily. Many people are accustomed to "thinking" about feelings instead of being and feeling with our bodies. The simple act of being with the felt sense allows for shifts and changes in immediate experience. Being with the now experience always opens to something new.

Practice Step 5: Now, staying with the felt sense, ask yourself how this whole experience connects to something going on in your life.

Carrying forward. A felt sense neither pushes nor pulls us toward the future; instead, the totality of the feeling, thought, and image received as a whole suggests or implies a way forward. Our work is to follow it. My pastoral experience leads me to suspect that coming into contact with a wider dimension of ourselves and God's mysterious presence open previously unimagined horizons.

Practice Step 6: Receive with gratitude any new insight or perspective. Take any next steps that seem appropriate.

Chapter 4

Freeing the Prisoner

Focusing is a practice for people and communities "on the go." It is a brief form of therapy, from the Greek word *therapeia* meaning "to serve," that can be done in only a few minutes with careful attention, and its benefits can be felt immediately. We only need willingness to give attention and to listen. We serve our own and others' wholeness and well-being through this hospitable body practice. Dogged determination to "get rid of" what bothers us has a boomerang effect: the body senses this attitude and fights back through increased agitation and restlessness. Focusing allows us to befriend our bodies and the messages they carry. There is a caution as well: focusing is a therapeutic "check-in" practice, not a quick fix. Joe's story clues us in to the process.

Joe wrestled with feelings of humiliation at being overlooked for a job promotion. He kept up the self-interrogation, which was different versions of the same question: "What could I have done differently to change the outcome?" Joe replayed the "givens" of the situation: institutional culture and retrenchment of senior leadership. As his pastoral counselor, I had to process my thoughts and feelings since his experience paralleled my own from earlier in my career. It was initially hard for Joe to own his anger and frustration, and I could see that as the only way through. But it was his work to do. He wanted to externalize or get rid of it. The feelings kept boomeranging: they reappeared in different guises such as annoyance with organizational processes at his local church.

Acceptance is hard. But Joe worked at it. Little shifts occurred over time. The intensity of the anger gradually subsided, and the tension in his back softened. No big "breakthroughs" occurred. At times, it all felt slow and plodding. All the while, Joe was doing his "body work"—daily meditation, journaling, biking, and playing basketball. He learned to be more at ease with living in what he perceived as "the mess of it all." He stopped looking outside for answers and instead grew more adept at focusing inside for clues. In so doing, he discovered and developed an internal pathway for sensing instead of thinking his way through life's ups and downs.

Focusing helps open the internal doorway to freedom with our bodies. "Here" in this liminal or threshold space, we encounter ourselves more fully. "Here" in this experience, we meet God, even if the past keeps pulling us back. Each moment of experience presents opportunity toward something new. Focusing helps us to stop and to check in with the creative work underway in our bodies. We are asked not to change the inherent blessing of who God created us to be, but to tap into the transformation underway. Focusing is a practice of getting in touch with what really matters *for us*.

Introducing body-focusing exercises can feel emotionally risky in some contexts. We may be worried that others will be critical and hesitant to engage. We might find, though, that our worry gives way to deep appreciation as colleagues, clients, and parishioners welcome the experiential learning. Experience has taught me to allow people options in how they can participate and opt out. It is important to honor and respect unease, hesitancy, and resistance. It helps also to be aware that oppressed and marginalized people may not feel they have the choice not to participate. For some people, the only choice is a forced one: internalized expectations prompt participation to keep others from noticing and judging. We might not necessarily know at this moment how our choices have been limited. Teachers and leaders need to recognize how difficult it may be for some people to exercise choice. Ideology and oppressive systems take up residence within us. Social oppression lives internally in the minds and bodies of the oppressed, holding us hostage even when the door is open.

Body Care Prayer

Breath of God, form a new and fresh spirit within us. Make us attentive to our inward being, even as we recognize our anxiety and fear of encountering the not-yet-familiar. May we stay with You and stay with ourselves just a little while longer. In this lingering space, allow us to make friends with ourselves as we synch with the rhythm of *ruah*, Your Breath of Life. We pause, sense, and embrace the newness of life that stirs within and among us. We say yes and follow. Amen.

Chapter 5
SENSING THE SACRED

A parishioner shared a story of having extreme pain in her wrist and being in need of a cortisone shot. When the physician took her hand to administer the shot, Joan found herself welling up with tears. It felt good to be touched on the hand and know someone cared. Every day, we meet people in need of touch. Maybe we ourselves need touch. In the age of widespread social media, people live with touch deprivation. Touching and being touched is a basic human need that extends throughout our lives. We are wired for being connected to others.

As spiritual leaders and seekers, we participate in God's healing as we connect with body senses. This has benefits for people in our care, like Joan, and for our faith walk, too. We are, of course, always navigating the world through use of our senses, but we are not necessarily attentive to the rich texture of learning about ourselves, others, and God that occurs. We benefit from becoming aware of the information that comes through our senses and how we meet God, others, and ourselves through this awareness.

Christianity is a body religion for people hungering for connection. Our bodies are God's temple, we hear. Instead of this being a freeing message, though, it can become a stumbling block. Sara, a twenty-two-year-old on the cusp of graduating from college, detests the phrase "the body as the temple of God." She explains: "Because I associate temples with holiness and purity, I have always felt that this placed another requirement on me. I thought I had to be pure. I thought my body had to be pure. It feels like a pressured requirement." Sara's apprehension and fear may be ours, too, especially if we have experienced social stereotyping and marginalization.

I don't want to argue Sara or anyone else out of their association with an image. Our experience matters. But an encounter with temples and cathedrals offers other possibilities. In Scotland, I learned that the walls of the abbey church in Iona were made to breathe. Ferns grow in walls. Birds take flight in the sanctuary. Light shines through the windows. Incense burns. People share in conversation, prayer, and singing. It is a place that fills the senses and glorifies God. Our work in care and faith is to rework images and practices to make room for the goodness of our bodies. We need to dispense with the images that hinder us. Instead, we need to explore how our body senses open pathways to experiencing God and offering care.

As we have explored, in the Hebrew Bible, the word used for compassion is "womb love." In the New Testament, Jesus has compassion for the disciples. The word for compassion describes "feeling in the gut." In Buddhism, a koan (a paradoxical riddle) states that the bodhisattva of compassion not only *has* eyes and hands but also *is* eyes and hands.[1] Compassion has an immediacy and tactile quality to it. Compassion is care in action. We do not "think" compassion and then act, but rather we "think" and "act" compassion simultaneously. We practice compassion by connecting with the whole of our bodies, including our senses.

Holy Touch

Touch is the most immediate of the body senses. "It can bring you in from the false world, the famine world of exile and image. Rediscovering the sense of touch returns you to the hearth of your own spirit, enabling you to experience again warmth, tenderness, and belonging," writes John O'Donohue.[2] Yet fear and confusion can get in the way. Our personal histories may include abuse, neglect, rejection, and trauma. This makes

---

1. "Case 89," *The Blue Cliff Record*, trans. Thomas Cleary and J.C. Cleary (Boston: Shambhala Publications, 1977). I thank Sensei Susan Kodo Efird for her talks (teishos) that have opened for me new avenues of spiritual exploration.

2. John O'Donohue, *Anam Cara: A Book of Celtic Wisdom* (New York: Harper Perennial, 1998), 75.

touch a difficult subject to consider. Churches and religious communities convey conflicting messages regarding bodies and touch. So, no doubt, this is a tricky matter.

Touch is sacred because our bodies are molded by God from the dirt and clay of the earth. "It is mysterious that the human body is clay. The individual is the meeting place of the four elements."[3] As we pay attention to our bodies, we connect with the earth. Touch becomes sacred as we engage with integrity, respect, and recognition of appropriate relational boundaries. Touch is a source of connection. Touch stimulates growth and development in early life. Touch makes us feel real.

> **Practicing Touch with the Earth**
>
> Here are practices of touch with the earth:
>
> - planting and tending a garden;
> - hiking or strolling or rolling or sitting outdoors;
> - removing your shoes and feeling the floor or ground underneath.
>
> Use your imagination. How do you touch the earth? Touching the earth is a safe means of building confidence and trust. If we start the practices alone, it might be a good idea to find ways to connect with others. Take it one step at a time and see what works.

Touch is a complex subject as indicated by current research. Neuroscientist David Linden goes beyond saying touch is good and important and teaches about its intricacies. We desire touch in some instances and do not want or welcome it in others. We want touch from some people and not from others. Touch involves "body circuits, from the skin to nerves to the brain . . . a weird, complex, and often counterintuitive [system], and the specifics of its organization powerfully influence our lives."[4] Science informs our thinking about and adhering to good practices with touch. We seek to help and not to harm. Touch is a form of "social glue" that

---

3. O'Donahue, *Anam Cara*, 92.
4. David J. Linden, *Touch: The Science of the Hand, Heart, and Mind* (New York: Penguin, 2016), 5.

connects us through the organ of our skin.⁵ We all differ in our needs and desires. We give and receive touch in different ways depending on who we are and how and where we grew up. A researcher observed people in cafes in different countries to see how often they touched each other. The results are striking: in Puerto Rico, touch occurred 180 times per hour; in Paris, 110 times per hour; in Gainesville, Florida, 2 times per hour; in London, no touch occurred.⁶ Cafes are not churches or spiritual communities. Still, the study prompts **questions:** To what degree is touch encouraged/permissible in your culture? What do you do if you are a high touch person in a low touch context? Or vice versa: a low touch person in a high touch context? What helps to reduce miscommunication and misunderstanding? Touch always occurs in context that also determines its personal and social meaning.⁷

We feel touch differently depending on the nature of the relationship and the situation in which it occurs. The social and verbal messages surrounding touch change how touch is experienced.⁸ In my early years on the faculty, I distinctly remember a colleague putting an arm around my shoulder in a meeting and saying, "Michael will take care of this." The gesture felt patronizing and made me angry. I did not welcome the touch because of the message it conveyed both to me and to others present: I did not feel lifted up as a leader but rather diminished. At times, touch or being inside the zone of another person's personal space is experienced as a violation. We do not just "reach out and touch somebody." Instead, we use caring language together with requesting permission before touching others.

Just because we want to provide touch does not mean another person welcomes it. This point is illustrated beautifully in a video on training volunteers for visitation.⁹ In caring and healing environments, we lead

---

5. See Linden, *Touch*, 9.
6. See Linden, *Touch*, 96.
7. Linden, *Touch*, 31.
8. Linden, *Touch*, 32.
9. The video "Communicating with Compassion" is free to watch at www.adventuresincaring.org/communicating-with-compassion-the-video/.

by observing the cues of others. If someone reaches out a hand, then they are probably comfortable with a handshake. If someone reaches out with open arms, they are sending a signal of being comfortable with a hug. If we are not good at reading social cues, then we need to ask permission and wait for a response. We need to respect the other person by graciously receiving a "no, thank you" when necessary.

Touch is sacred practice when it reinforces positive emotions. If touch makes people or ourselves feel anxious or troubled, then we need to refrain from it. When offered and received with permission and grace, touch tells others they are good and beloved beings. People feel cared for and loved. Never should we use touch to cultivate a sexual or intimately inappropriate relationship in ministry. We must take care of our own touch needs outside of professional and lay caregiving relationships to maintain ethical relational boundaries.

Touch might not always make good sense in local congregations. A longtime member of a church I served disliked holding hands during the benediction. It seemed curious since Bert would happily shake hands after church or touch some people on the shoulder during conversations. The topic came up at a church council meeting, and he said, "I don't know. I just don't like it." Sometimes, it is just like that. Hopefully spiritual communities can make room for all people: those who like and want touch, and those who may be hesitant or resistant. Create opportunities for people to exercise choice.

Touch and Care

Small gestures make a big difference. How can we do this? Again, the key is to follow the other person's lead and always be respectful:

Sharing a handshake with two hands instead of just one

Hugging another person with permission, preferably with others present

Touching lightly on the wrist, forearm, or shoulder

Chapter 5

Real and Virtual Worlds

When a colleague was diagnosed with cancer, I was especially grateful to get updates through an online site.[10] This online venue allowed people to stay connected with the family and offer words of support throughout his treatment. Online resources offer tremendous benefits to share information widely with people, avoid the burden of repetition, and solicit help with care such as respite visits (giving family members time away to tend to other life needs), home or pet care, and meal preparation, among others.

Sensible and sense-filled care keeps focus on physical, embodied presence. We do well to envision online resources and physical presence as complements and not substitutes. Jaco Hamman explores how the use of technology reflects and shapes how we understand and relate with one another and with God. The presence and use of technology cannot be avoided, and new tools become available at a rapid pace. Hamman discusses different "intelligences" to "grow down" as we learn how and when to use and not to use technology.[11] Caregivers and churches can reflect intentionally on if, how, and when to use technological resources in support of spiritual care practices, recognizing both the possibilities and limits that each form of technology presents. Individuals and communities need to make decisions for care plans that make sense. When we are ill, suffering, or grieving, we might need to be alone or only with people whose presence makes us comfortable. We might spend time with body senses: watching a windmill, listening to music, lighting incense, caressing with essential oils, giving or receiving massage. Just as we "grow up," we also need to "grow down" in order to live into our full humanity. We must learn to set aside technology when it becomes "addictive substitute" and to live into our identity as God's beloved creations.

We can practice embodied care through responsive listening using a variety of media. Whether we are in-person or using technology to interact, the key is to minimize distractions and give our full attention.

---

10. See, for example, www.caringbridge.com, as well as Facebook and online condolence sites.

11. Jaco J. Hamman, *Growing Down: Theology and Human Nature in the Virtual Age* (Waco, TX: Baylor University Press, 2017).

Through open and available presence, we sit together, feel emotions, see body language, and connect with wet tears. In an age of the instantaneous and superficial, our bodies yearn for sustained relationship. Depending on our life stage and circumstances, we may prefer one mode of connection over another. Caregivers can tailor the mode of communication depending on the care seeker's preference and availability. Especially in care with senior adults, body presence offers vital social connection to reduce the sense of isolation and loneliness. Animals can provide helpful care through their physical presence within institutional settings. Dogs and cats especially can help patients by reducing anxiety and calming fears.[12] The animal companions provide tactile connection. For many people and especially for those who have been pet owners, stroking the fur on a dog or hearing the purring of a cat has healing effects on the body. We are all, human and animals alike, companions in presence and mediators of God's presence as we practice embodied care in ways that make practical sense. It matters when we show up at a funeral, walk through a greeting line, hug a friend or loved one, touch a hand or shoulder, and shed and wipe away tears together. We meet as embodied souls and spirits to bear witness to our tangible, material lives.

Our Senses in Grief and Pain

In grief, people may feel as if they are falling apart. We sometimes consciously and often unconsciously push grief away. It is a lot of work to go through the grieving process. Grieving takes physical and emotional energy. Grieving is an intense bodily practice of letting go. "My tears have been my food both day and night, as people constantly questioned me, 'Where's your God now?'" (Ps 42:3), laments the psalmist.

Janet's body story of grief shows how connected her grieving is with her body senses. The body pain associated with a contentious divorce left her questioning her self-esteem and the possibility of loving again. She talked in our pastoral care conversations about her night laments. She

---

12. Michael S. Koppel, "Companions in Presence: Animal Assistants and Eldercare," *Pastoral Psychology* 60:1 (2011): 107–15.

would go to bed and lie awake. She could feel pain and grief in her body and would be unable to hold it back any longer. The grief would erupt in thunderous rolling waves with her chest heaving and tears streaming down her face. Feeling spent from the waves of grief, she would then notice herself feeling the supportive comfort of the bed. She seemed more open to the silence of the night and felt enveloped in the orchestra of sound coming from crickets and cicadas. She noticed the feel and smell of her cool breath. Grieving exhausted her and made her feel more alive, both at the same time. Janet did not want the grief and yet could not deny how it opened body senses.

The psalmist captures how grief cascades through the body. Tears are soul food, in a strange and yet deeply familiar way. Tears feed the soul for the psalmist and feed our souls as well in a bitterly satisfying way. Tears, at least, provide a release of the grief sometimes held tightly within. Grieving is a deeply physical experience. A parishioner described the "physically exhausting" grief following a family member's death. He would stand in the shower for an hour or longer, a body practice expressing a physical inner desire for the water to substitute for the tears that at various times flowed uncontrollably or would not flow at all. On the other side of grief, in the moments of the day when emotion was held at bay, he enjoyed the sight and fragrance of flowers blooming in the garden.

Body senses connect us with God. The senses provide a "secure base" that keeps us grounded.[13] A secure base is the confidence that we are held, known, embraced, and cared for in this very moment. We might have memories of a positive childhood that reinforce our confidence. Some people spend years developing this inner capacity that was not adequately nurtured by others in early life. Body senses ground us and connect us with God's presence. In times of difficulty, we may want to flee our bodies, but it is just the opposite that is needed: we need to find practices to stay grounded.

Grief shows up differently in each person's body. We also have preferences for senses that ground us.

---

13. John Bowlby, *A Secure Base: Parent-Child Attachment and Healthy Human Development* (New York: Basic Books, 1988).

Floodgates: Some people hold back the floodgate of tears until they cannot stop them any longer. The grief wells inside and manifests as tension, anger, and frustration. It can feel like a force we are trying desperately to hold back. Grief can also present as a general haze of dissatisfaction.

Malaise: A colleague names grief as "malaise," a lack of energy and enthusiasm. It is not the same kind of low as clinical depression.

Sleepwalking: Grief can make us feel as if we are sleepwalking. We sense ourselves "here" and "not here."

Going through the motions: Grief can feel like we are "treading molasses"; every act takes effort.

The Physicality of Grief

Psalm 22:14-15 captures the physical aspects of grief: "I'm poured out like water. All my bones have fallen apart. My heart is like wax; it melts inside me. My strength is dried up like a piece of broken pottery. My tongue sticks to the roof of my mouth; you've set me down in the dirt of death." This psalm is saturated with body metaphors. The images capture our body sensations and invite our further reflection. How is your grief like being "poured out like water" or "like wax"? How is the body grieving? Can we allow ourselves to be one with our body experience and not resist it? Physical aspects of grief play out differently for each of us. We connect with some images and not with others. We are soothed through the senses: listening to a harp, smelling the aroma of food baking or cooking, seeing a beautiful sunrise or sunset, petting the dog.

> **Question:** When you experience grief by (1) holding back, (2) having low energy, and (3) going through the motions, what body senses help you connect with yourself and others?

Chapter 5

Body Care and Tears

God models body care and touch by receiving our tears. Consider the following prayer adapted from Psalm 56:8-11:

O God of our tears,
>You have kept count of our tossings.

Put our tears in your bottle.
Are they not in your record?
>In God, whose word we praise,
>
>In the Lord, whose word we praise,
>
>In God we trust. We are not afraid. Amen.[14]

God is in touch by collecting human tears and putting them in God's bottle. This gesture of poignant intimacy portrays divine empathic presence with the body. Such interactive and touching care can be ritualized between caregivers and care recipients and within care-group settings in congregations and classrooms. Expressions and needs of the body are not secondary or instrumental concerns to God but are primary. What the body presents is always real, not abstract. Certainly, it is possible to fake tears or pretend anger or feign joy, but other bodies can "read" such fabrications. Like a good therapist, God tracks and remembers our body story and stores it in God's memory bank or "bottle."

> **Group Exercise:** Choose a vessel with an opening that can represent God's bottle in Psalm 56. Play background music. On cut-out pieces of paper in the shape of tears, write down an experience of grief or loss. Drop the "tears" into God's "bottle." After everyone has "shed tears," join together in reciting Psalm 56.[15]

---

14. Denise Dombkowski Hopkins and Michael S. Koppel, *Grounded in the Living Word: The Old Testament and Pastoral Care Practices* (Grand Rapids: Eerdmans, 2010), 147.

15. Dombkowski Hopkins and Koppel, *Grounded in the Living Word*, 147

Serving through the Senses

We know and serve God through our body senses. The early church knew this, and the Bible certainly affirms it. Acts 13 records that the church at Antioch commissioned Barnabas and Saul to preach: "After they fasted and prayed, they laid their hands on these two and sent them off" (v. 3). In the Gospels, Jesus is portrayed as washing the disciples' feet as a form of hospitality. His willingness to touch feet, the body's lowest part, signifies his commitment to serve even the least of these. Mary Magdalene "anointed the Lord with fragrant oil and wiped his feet with her hair" (John 11:2) as a full expression of devotion. In learning of Lazarus's death, "Jesus began to cry" (John 11:35); tear-shedding was his body's response to loss of relationship. The psalmist sings of tasting divine life: "Taste and see how good the Lord is! The one who takes refuge in him is truly happy!" (Ps 34:8). Hearing and listening means knowing that God is whole, and our faith practice includes welcoming our wholeness: "Israel, listen! Our God is the Lord! Only the Lord!" (Deut 6:4).

The Bible passages showcase our senses as vehicles of faith. In our daily lives, we can mirror such practices in creative and imaginative ways. When leading a college retreat one weekend in the spring, I cut fresh flowers from the front yard to place in a vase in the classroom. I had never done this before. The idea was prompted by my reflection on our leadership theme for the weekend: practicing leadership in community with head, hearts, and hands. We needed stimulation for the senses.

Anointing is a practice that relates to bodily senses. In the Hebrew Bible or the Old Testament, anointing channels God's life force and favor into the one being anointed. David and Saul both receive anointing for their kingships, and their reigns flourish at least initially because God has had a hand in them. First Samuel 10:1: "Samuel took a small jar of oil and poured it over Saul's head and kissed him. 'The Lord hereby anoints you leader of his people Israel,' Samuel said." Notice the senses: *smell* (the vial of oil), *feel* it on the skin, receive the *touch* of a kiss, *hear* the words of blessing, and in the implied sense, *see* this happen before you.

An overflow of life energy is associated with the anointing. Saul falls in with a band of ecstatic prophets: "And just as Saul turned to leave Samuel's side, God gave him [Saul] a different heart, and all these signs happened that very same day. When Saul and the boy got to Gibeah, there was a group of prophets coming to meet him. God's spirit came over Saul, and he was caught up in a prophetic frenzy right along with them" (1 Sam 10:9-10). God's energy ignites Saul's whole body, driving him into this "prophetic frenzy." In Zen Buddhism, the word *joriki* is akin to turning on the electricity in the body. *Alive, electric, energized* all describe the senses being open.

Gentle Body Rituals

We can incorporate gentle body rituals in our lives and care situations. These practices may include tending and anointing foreheads, hands, and feet. Modifications may be necessary depending on the context and level of comfort. If, for instance, people are culturally not accustomed to foot washing, consideration can be given to washing hands or blessing foreheads instead. Aromatherapy is a modern practice with ancient religious roots. Application of essence oils on the hands or the forehead during care conversation or in a worship setting can be especially touching for those who choose to participate. Exercise wise caution with these practices. Check to ensure people do not have allergies that would cause adverse reactions.

> **Questions for Reflection:** Our senses can grow dull through familiarity and habit. We may not fully taste, touch, smell, hear, and feel. Yet, God's energy beckons to flow through us. How can you strengthen attention to your senses? "How much lightning can you stand?"[16]

Body Senses and Relationships

Body senses come to our aid in mending relationships. The Bible showcases what this looks like in practice. After years apart, estranged

---

16. Ann Belford Ulanov, *Knots and Their Untying: Essays on Psychological Dilemmas* (Einsiedein, Switzerland: Daimon Verlag, 2020). See "How Much Lightning Can We Stand?" 69–86.

brothers Jacob and Esau reunite in a bear hug. "But Esau *ran* to meet him, *threw his arms around* his neck, *kissed* him, and they *wept*" (Gen 33:4, italics added). The action suggests engagement of the senses even though they are not all named explicitly: seeing, running, embracing (threw his arms around), kissing, and weeping. Imagine yourself there and how your senses would be engaged. The brothers have been out of touch for years. We imagine their bodies feel the effects of separation. Mending relationships takes strength and vulnerability in differing measures from each person. Esau, whose birthright was stolen by his brother Jacob, runs toward his brother and "[bows] to the ground seven times" as an embodied gesture of humility and respect (Gen 33:3). We know authenticity—whether people are being real or not—when we see, hear, touch, feel, and smell it. Our body story and practices of care draw on the wisdom of the senses.

Genesis 2 is an "earthy" contrast to the majestic order of Genesis 1. Consider the creation of human beings in Genesis 2:7 (NRSV): "[T]hen the Lord God formed man from the dust of the ground, and breathed into his nostrils the breath of life; and the man became a living being." Human being is of the earth and deeply entwined in Divine Spirit. God determined 'adam needed a companion: "It is not good that the man should be alone; I will make him a helper as his partner" (Gen 2:18 NRSV). The man goes into a "deep sleep," and one of his ribs (actually "side") is removed and then his side is closed up again. The Hebrew word for rib actually means to "come out of the side." The image and language suggest mutuality: companion, partner, and beloved describe the relationship being depicted. We arise from the clay of the earth, connected with one another and enlivened through God's spirit to form relationships and care for creation. We use the senses endowed to us by God to connect to God, ourselves, and one another. We expand the creation story through our own bodies and senses by continuing to expand our imaginations, exploring the boundaries of what is possible, and following our curiosity to transform God's beloved creation.[17]

---

17. In my view, these sensibilities and practices belong to all human beings, including women and men and others. For analysis of the creation story, see Anne W. Stewart, "Eve and Her Interpreters" in *Women's Bible Commentary*, 46–50.

Love Lingers

After a premarital conversation in my office, I turned to other tasks. Each time upon leaving and returning to the office, I noticed faint hints of perfume. The following Sunday, I preached on the passage in which Mary wipes Jesus's feet with expensive perfume. "Then Mary took an extraordinary amount, almost three-quarters of a pound, of very expensive perfume made of pure nard. She anointed Jesus' feet with it, then wiped his feet dry with her hair. The house was filled with the aroma of the perfume" (John 12:3). The sermon was entitled "A Generous Pour" and written before the conversation in my office. The focus was on Mary's intimate devotional practice. While preaching, I recalled the experience of perfume lingering in my office. I now had visceral knowledge of the passage in a way I did not have previously. I gained theological insight into a biblical passage through connection to a body sense. Gestures of love linger. Mary offers her intimate prayer to Jesus and the scent of perfume lingers for millennia. When we give to God the closest and costliest parts of ourselves, the scent of the act pervades the whole house. We ourselves are affected and so is the surrounding community. Love lingers . . . for real.

Seeing Faith

Senses also fail and faith is tried. John sat down for our advising appointment to go over the courses he planned to take the next semester. I asked how he was doing. John lives with an eye disease that has affected him since he was twelve years old. At seventeen, he lost his sight completely. Through medical treatment, he regained some of his sight. In midlife, he still copes with the eye disease. Instead of a precipitous drop into blindness, as was the case when John was seventeen, every day he awakes and adjusts to his sight level for that day. It is a daily struggle because the disease itself causes pain. He never knows how well he will be able to see.

John is a poet and speaks eloquently about his relationship with the disease. "Chronic illness," he says, "is like having a life partner. It's always there. So, it helps to have a good connection." John speaks knowingly of this relationship. "It is important, I find, to have a comfortable understanding of the disease since it is always with me." John's words are easy to hear, but I imagine getting to this place took immense effort. A "comfortable understanding" suggests body awareness forged through many hard days and nights with emotional ups and downs. John prefers the way of understanding instead of the way of fighting. "Fighting drains my essence," he says.

John had a counselor for the blind who was helpful to him in his teen years. John internalized the counselor's words: "You have the opportunity to learn a lot about yourself." He found the words meaningful. As an adult, he told a good friend what the counselor said. This friend, optimistic and positive, thought the counselor's words were ridiculous. Perhaps the friend does not grasp what John knows about himself. The disease has indelibly shaped him. It is part of his identity. He has come to see and to embrace aspects of himself that he loves. While not grateful for the disease, John is aware of knowing himself deeply because of it.

John's prayer of lament shares the rawness of his pain and struggle and the deep yearning of his heart. His lament—soul cry—expresses an intimacy with and yearning for God. He has learned about God and himself and promises to be a teacher by helping others "to see."

John's Lament

God of light, creator of light, bring your creation to me once more.
With the dawning of each day
You have shown my eyes new light
After lifting me out of deep darkness.
Now your revelation of morning light
Opens a door to constant pain and struggle.
Is there a reason why you have me spiraling back to darkness, my LORD?
Am I not appreciative of your gift?
Do I not acknowledge the beauty of your creations in my prayers?
Lead me to light once more, my LORD, lead me to light.
I am faithful, my LORD, I am worthy of your light.
Each day I open my eyes knowing full well that you
Produced a miracle of new light for me before.
You gave me new light as a child after one thousand days of blindness.

I have learned much to teach others about your gift
Lead me to light once more, my LORD, lead me to light.[18]

So may we appreciate the gift of body senses as a pathway to the Divine and a healing connection with others.

Eye-Gazing Practice

"Eye-gazing" practice draws on the sense of sight.[19] We practice staying present as we meditate, as we gaze into another person's eyes. We allow ideas, judgments, evaluations, thoughts, and feelings to rise up and fall away. We focus on cultivating gentle presence through breathing and gazing.

At least three people are needed for the practice: two people to engage the practice and one to initiate it and observe the time. People need to feel free to participate or not, since the practice can feel too awkward or close for some. Initially, a period of ten minutes is sufficient.

(1) Sit on a chair or on a cushion so that both people are at the same eye level.

(2) Knees should be close but not touching.

(3) Keep eyes focused downward until the attendant signals the start (by ringing a bell or chime).

(4) When the practice session begins, focus on breathing and gazing into one of the other person's eyes. The practice is not about locking eyes or staring.

(5) Reflect together on your experience.

Mirror Eye-Gazing

Mirror eye-gazing is a practice I have adapted for practicing alone. We practice being compassionately present with ourselves. So often, we

---

18. Publishing permission is granted by John M. Lewis..

19. Steve Smith of the Claremont Meditation Group introduced me to this practice.

become habituated to looking at ourselves as "objects" in need of correction. We may stand in front of a mirror and immediately look for faults: wrinkled skin, circles under the eyes, bad hair, breakouts, blemishes. We evaluate and judge our bodies. Mirror eye-gazing invites us to see, appreciate, and value ourselves and our bodies, looking past the imperfections.

The practice enhances body and self-acceptance. We might observe tears welling up or see the "whole of our face" even while focused on gazing. We practice the great commandment with our bodies through our eyes: to love with all our heart, mind, and soul.

Body Care Prayer

God of Body and Soul,
This day, I make commitment to care for self and others in ways that honor body integrity. I vow to give and receive appropriate touch. I vow to listen and speak stories with authentic truth. I vow to stay present when difficult emotions arise. I vow to eat and drink modestly and wisely. I vow to make space for exercise and movement. I vow not to turn away from whatever I consider least or lost in the world. I vow to learn about you and serve others appropriately and ethically by tending to gifts of body senses. Amen.

Chapter 6

SILENT PRAYER THROUGH OUR BODIES

On the last day of a silent prayer retreat, Rick had an overwhelming sense of being wrapped in love. Energy radiated throughout his body. The experience surprised him. When we met Katherine, the residential spiritual director, he spontaneously hugged her and said, "I love you." Even though they had known each other for years, Rick's spontaneous gesture caught Katherine off guard. Her body stiffened in response to the hug. Rick wrote Katherine a letter of apology. In a subsequent conversation, she simply said, "You are forgiven." Rick wondered whether Katherine was serious or joking. He never raised the subject again.

Silent prayer may not be suitable for everyone, but it can open God's energizing spirit to the hearts of those inclined to practice. In Rick's story above, prayer catalyzed a desire to reach out and connect with those he admired and trusted. For Katherine touching was not considered taboo but was clearly an uncomfortable practice, perhaps related to her family and religious upbringing. God's creative spirit nevertheless gifted her with a wry sense of humor. When she said to Rick, "You are forgiven," she did so with a playful lilt in her voice. We can imagine such interactions in our lives. There is not one ideal way of bearing the fruit of God's spirit experienced in silence. While silence connects body and spirit with God, we each express and envision that reality differently.

Chapter 6

Contemplative Spiritual Care

Our lives are gifts to receive and not projects to endure. Silence allows the body "to be" in its natural state, not having to carry out projects created in our minds that can lead to endless busyness and little calm. In this chapter, we explore how silent prayer enlivens and nurtures our bodies. Silence is a word to name "reality without words," where our bodies encounter God. However, I want to offer a cautionary note up front: silence might frighten people who have experienced trauma. If the thought of silence and prayer stirs apprehension, anxiety, or fear, then it is best to pay attention to these signals and be gentle with oneself and not proceed with silent prayer practices. Trauma may have occurred when the body was relaxed and quiet.

Sand settling to the bottom of the ocean can capture the experience of quiet prayer. With many thoughts (sand) floating in the mind and emotions (sand) igniting in the body, we can sense all that is unsettled as we sit and pray in silence. We sometimes may want to figure out what's going on by thinking and stewing about it! This is an inner current of resistance. What's needed is recognizing and releasing the sand in God's presence, and gradually the body experiences being calm, restful, and alive. Howard Thurman describes the experience of quiet prayer as "rest" in "the Great Silence," in which "God speaks without words and the self listens without ears."[1] Poet Denise Levertov names her own longing for this encounter with God as her "bones ached for silence."[2] **Reflect for yourself:** What image or phrase names your body experience with silence?

I realize the irony of talking about silence. One wonders why so much language is needed to describe being quiet! The irony is further compounded by all the nuances generated to name and describe the underlying processes of silence. They include centering prayer, contemplative practice, meditation, apophatic prayer, being/sitting in silence, prayer of the heart, and nondualism. Language is a vehicle for expression and often seems inadequate to capture an experience of "connection," "loving and

---

1. Howard Thurman, *The Inward Journey* (Richmond, IN: Friends United, 1961), 112.
2. Interview at a poetry reading at Cornell University, 1993.

being loved," "knowing and being known," "facing our true selves before God," and so on. In fact, you will encounter language variations in this chapter. Realize this: language is a form of power and can be used to open new possibilities or to shut them down. The use of language is intended to help readers love God and foster awareness.[3] Encounter God in beautiful, mysterious silence, and notice the experience in your body.

We don't need to abandon our theological views or beliefs in order to practice in silence. But we might notice changes in our theology over time as we discover ourselves less self-centered or obsessed and more God-centered in our approach to life. Silence awakens and energizes us from the inside out.

Contemplative spiritual care promotes embodied wholeness as it begins in, stays with, and returns to the body. We are certainly "so *much more* than just this body, just this personal drama," as Ezra Bayda asserts about the purpose of our lives and spiritual practice.[4] We are also *nothing* without our bodies. Our embodiment is a living paradox.[5] Spiritual care with the body should neither make an idol of the body nor undermine the body. In the Christian tradition, care springs from respectful love, which mirrors God's own love for the world by becoming embodied in Jesus Christ, the One who is fully human and fully divine. This theological vision undergirds contemplative practice. Barbara Holmes uses "contemplative" to name a broad diversity of practices within the Black Church tradition that "can be silent or evocative, still or embodied in dance and shout" that consistently attend "to the Spirit of God."[6] Throughout the chapter, the term *contemplative* is used to describe intentional practices of being intimate with and responding to God through our bodies.

---

3. Thomas Keating writes: "Eastern methods are primarily concerned with awareness. Centering Prayer is concerned with divine love." In *Intimacy with God: An Introduction to Centering Prayer* (New York: Crossroad, 2009), 147.

4. Ezra Bayda, *Being Zen: Bringing Meditations to Life* (Boston: Shambhala, 2002), 141–42, emphasis added.

5. For women and men spiritual seekers inclined toward meditative practice, the following book explores this paradox in greater detail. See *Being Bodies: Buddhist Women on the Paradox of Embodiment*, eds. Lenore Friedman and Susan Moon (Boston: Shambhala, 1997).

6. Barbara A. Holmes, *Joy Unspeakable: Contemplative Practices of the Black Church*, 2nd ed. (Minneapolis: Fortress, 2017), 5.

Contemplative practices create space and support justice for all bodies. Such practices do not necessarily occur in silence; when they do, we need to be aware of both negative and positive dimensions of silence. Negative uses of silence and contemplative practices include reinforcing a rigid form of self-denial, holding to strict external rules with no room for flexibility, and withholding helpful and healing words. The positive uses of silence and contemplative practice include opening our bodies, minds, and hearts to God's life within and around; building trust and confidence in the body for faithful action; and creating and nurturing contexts in which bodies can flourish.

> **Questions:** When/how have you experienced either a positive or negative use of silence in your life? How did that experience make you feel? What do you notice in your body as you reflect on this question?

Covenant Theology and Practice

Creating contexts within which all bodies can flourish is one of the foundations for covenant relationship. Covenant provides the "vision for social and individual life" for people who are "making sense of the world and their place in it."[7] "The covenant that God makes with Israel is perhaps the central and defining theological affirmation of the Old Testament. The covenant is at the same time a theological affirmation, liturgic practice, and a durable public institution in Israel."[8] Covenant is a "bilateral commitment" between God and God's people and among God's people in relationship.[9] Paul calls the wine at the Eucharist "the new covenant" in Christ's blood (1 Cor 11:25). Covenant provides theological framing for embodied life with God. People of faith practice covenant loyalty by exercising responsibility for our own and other peoples' bodies.

---

7. Christopher D. Stanley, *Hebrew Bible: A Comparative Approach* (Minneapolis: Fortress, 2010), 190.

8. Walter Brueggemann, *Reverberations of Faith: A Theological Handbook of Old Testament Themes* (Louisville: Westminster John Knox, 2002), 37.

9. Denise Dombkowski Hopkins and Michael S. Koppel, *Grounded in the Living Word: The Old Testament and Pastoral Care Practices* (Grand Rapids: Eerdmans, 2010), 37.

Talking to and listening with God are both prayer forms that reflect covenant loyalty and draw on the body in different ways. Most people are familiar with prayer as "talking to God," a primary mode of expression in worship, and other rituals. We draw on our intellect, feelings, and imagination in this mode of prayer. "Listening with God" is a less familiar and yet transformative mode of prayer in which we tune in to the subtle spiritual perceptions experienced throughout our bodies.[10] Silence as a covenant practice puts us in touch with who we are and the depth and breadth of relationship with God and others. In silence, we tap the Source, and desire to embody covenant in words and actions. In silence, we experience being held so we can hold others in care.

> **Beginning Covenant Practice**
>
> Covenant "is a mutual agreement between people and God to take one another seriously in relationship."[11] We uphold covenant as we bring the whole of ourselves, not just parts of us, to relationship with God.
>
> **Questions:** What embodied quality are you tempted to "trade in"? What would be gained and what would be lost?

From Monastery to Daily Life

Into Great Silence captures the daily rhythms of life and prayer at a remote monastery in the French Alps.[12] Released in 2005, the film offers protracted snapshots of the monks: working in the garden, kneeling in bedrooms, eating at tables, getting haircuts, chanting together in worship, sitting in doorways, walking through the hallways. The monks do not speak on camera; the film has no dialogue or storyline to follow. Viewers also enter silence. The effect is meditative and mesmerizing. I was only disturbed by the sound of someone loudly eating popcorn and opening a can of soda in the theater! Without language to process, viewers find their attention drawn

---

10. Cynthia Bourgeault, *Centering Prayer and Inner Awakening* (Cambridge, MA: Cowley Publications, 2004), 36.
11. Dombkowski Hopkins and Koppel, *Grounded in the Living Word*, 205.
12. Philip Gronig, director. *Into Great Silence* (Zeitgeist Films, 2005).

to watching what the monks do, how they position their bodies and interact with other bodies. Absent the need to process speech, viewers are freed up to observe body language, including facial expressions.

A monastery provides structure for contemplative, silent prayer with God. We might assume it's an easy life, but the monks have their inner struggles. One monk bows in prayer repetitively. His face registers an intensity of emotion. Viewers sense he is wrestling with something significant. Viewers observe moments of sheer joy, too. The film concludes with the monks reveling in creation and taking delight in their bodies. The monks laugh as they play outside in the winter snow, taking turns sledding down a hill.

We aren't monks. However, we can make adjustments in our daily lives for silent prayer. We need to be intentional about setting a time and creating actual space for the practice. We can start by decluttering offices and homes. Marie Kondo has made a media splash with her mantra of keeping only those items that bring joy. General guidelines for claiming or reclaiming our homes and workplaces for prayer include getting rid of useless things, placing simple items of beauty in sight, and opening time in our schedules for being quiet. By doing so, we can minimize the noise of distractions and begin to foster communion with God in silence. We can create a "sanctuary" in our homes and/or offices, a physical environment that yet invites us to prayer.

Practice Point: Creating Sanctuary

The word *sanctuary* means "refuge" or "safety." Clearing or creating a physical space for prayer signals our intention to practice. The space need not be elaborate or large. Few people have rooms set aside for prayer and meditation. A favorite spot near a window, in a quiet room, on the balcony, or in the garden can be sanctuary space. Tangible items for inside spaces may include anything that draws toward presence with God such as an icon, cross, small statue of a saint or spiritual exemplar, candles, flowers, or fragrant oil or incense. For some people, an unadorned space free of sights and smells fosters a sense of retreat. Decide what suits you and your practice. How and where will you create your own space?

Once the space and place are set, we are ready to start our practice. But for some reason, we don't. We might walk by the area for many days and say, "I

> really should do that now." We think about how nice it would be and still avoid doing it. Why is this so? In part, the desire of our bodies needs time to convince our minds, even when it's an intention. We might notice the subtle resistances to being with God and ourselves in silence. Take care not to label these resistances as "excuses." That is the voice of the inner critic. Instead, recognize that practices take time to develop and take root in our lives.

Silence puts us in touch with our inner landscape and the fears that lurk there. At the same time, we both want and don't want to encounter them. We can hang in the ambivalence for a while, usually until we are forced into another perspective by life circumstances. We yearn for and resist silence because the stillness of our bodies and minds brings an association with death. We tend to keep ourselves in motion to avoid facing this reality. But the avoidance, too, causes pain and suffering. A spiritual director colleague often encouraged retreat participants with this message: "We are all in hospice together. We become intimate with dying." It was not at all a depressing or morose message, but a wake-up call to life. Quiet prayer when sustained as a regular practice fosters the ability to steer clear of distractions and trivial matters. This does not mean, however, that we ignore caring for practical matters that sustain livelihood and relationships. They, too, are part of keeping covenant. We practice in silence with our bodies to connect with the depth of faith: life, death, and resurrection.[13] In silence, we notice how we cling to the "not real," become addicted to unhealthy substances and practices, fuel fantasies, feed grievances, and replay old habits. Silent prayer helps to strip away the not real so we can live genuine lives before God. This parallels "the practice of mindfulness [that] can wake us up from a stupor of busyness and overstimulation."[14] Silence is a dive into deep connection in an information-driven, fast-paced, solution-focused world. Silence supports the body capacities of lingering, pondering, reflecting, wondering, and questioning.

Silence opens us to beauty. Without silence, there would be no music, which is the creative interplay between sound and silence. A

---

13. See Jean Stairs, *Listening for the Soul: Pastoral Care and Spiritual Direction* (Minneapolis: Augsburg Fortress, 2000).

14. See Amy Oden, *Right Here Right Now: The Practice of Christian Mindfulness* (Nashville: Abingdon Press, 2017), 2.

colleague who teaches church music is fond of saying, "No one leaves church humming the sermon!" In meditation and prayer, we tune ourselves in to silent music to grasp and to be grasped by life. Sitting still in silence is a gift to others in care as together we face the horizon of the possible.

> **Reflection Questions:** How comfortable are you with being in silence? Do you seek it or resist it? Why so?
>
> In what ways does your current life (schedule, environment, responsibilities) allow for contemplative silence? What are the hindrances?

> **Silence in a Noisy World:**
>
> Churches can help congregants and spiritual seekers nurture silence. Include periodic instructions and reflection in the church newsletter about contemplative practice (e.g., praying quietly, walking, drawing, and journaling); incorporate quotations from noted contemplatives in educational materials and worship bulletins (Thomas Merton, Teresa of Avila, and so on); give concrete suggestions in sermons and workshops for taking "pause breaks" in daily life; create drop-in times and space in the church for practice; make room for two minutes of silence in Sunday worship.

Living Wholeness

We have been blessed to be created human, a gift to be treasured and shared. The psalmist declares that you are "fearfully and wonderfully made," a resounding affirmation of our bodies (Ps 139:14 NRSV). Mary Oliver asks: "Tell me, what is it you plan to do with your one wild and precious life?"[15] Will you share or squander this gift? It's a shift for many people to see their blessing. We often operate from the self-negative and body-negative place: I'm no good; this body is flawed. Noted spiritual writer Henri Nouwen asserts, "Self-rejection is the greatest enemy of the spiritual life because it contradicts the sacred voice that calls us

---
15. Mary Oliver, "The Summer Day," in *New and Selected Poems, Vol. 1* (Boston: Beacon, 1992), 94.

'Beloved.'"[16] It's as if we stand in a palace of splendor and notice a picture hanging crooked on the wall. The self and body negativity impede our ability to receive the message of being the beloved. We sit in silent prayer as one practice to embrace our embodied identity and to hear truly: "You are fearfully and wonderfully made."

We also need other people as conversation partners to help us live into the wholeness God intends for us. Spiritual directors, pastors, religious teachers, and pastoral counselors can all be thoughtful companions as we discern our relationship with God through our bodies. Some people benefit from a formalized relationship developed with a skilled professional. We might seek such help and guidance at life junctures, perhaps in the beginning of a spiritual journey or during a critical transition. A formal relationship guarantees a care provider will devote primary attention to our needs and challenges as seekers of care.

In my experience, friends and colleagues can be thoughtful companions and interpreters of experience, provided sharing feels right for both and is not burdensome for either person. Those who are open and available to mutual relationship are most helpful. Sometimes, all we need is a brief conversation with a trusted person to help us "click" into awareness of body experience. This is a ministry that all people of faith as members of the body of Christ can fulfill. It is also the call of those devoted to living out their higher purpose for the planetary community. We do not need to cede our authority to people in positions of authority and power in order to be blessed, cleansed, healed, empowered, forgiven, and freed. Such is the responsibility of all members of the human family.

Discernment names an intentional reflective spiritual practice that can be utilized by individuals, groups, and institutions. We can describe discernment as a "capacity" that "implies both gift and skill in individuals and groups to recognize how God is operative in and around them."[17] We might use the phrase "I am in discernment" to mark a particular time or season for this sacred process that includes the embrace of our bodies to

---

16. Henri Nouwen, *Life of the Beloved: Spiritual Living in a Secular World* (New York: Crossroad), 28.

17. Elizabeth Liebert, SNJM, *The Soul of Discernment: A Spiritual Practice for Communities and Institutions* (Louisville: Westminster John Knox, 2015), 19.

discover what God is doing. As I write this, I watch children who have discovered the slope in my neighbor's yard. A decline invites a body roll, for the ones who exercise imagination and a flexible body. So there they go, rolling down the slope to the grassy area below. Children wouldn't think of leaving the body out. But as adults, we frequently tend to look past our bodies, and this is regretful especially when it comes to spiritual discernment. A couple of steps in the process include: (1) to "look, listen, and wait" on God, and (2) to take "next steps."[18] The first step of looking, listening, and waiting includes paying attention to the ordinary aspects of life. We encounter God in the "experience near" but often miss seeing divine activity at work because we expect a dramatic display. We can instead "look right here," which includes the overlooked aspects of our embodied experience. Taking a "next step" draws on the wisdom of the body. The reality is this: the body never lies. It is present, in silence and in speech, telling the truth.

Getting Started with Contemplative Practice

Honor your desire and be patient with your resistance to silence.

Prioritize time to practice prayerful listening. Choose a time that works for you. Start slowly. Choose two times during the coming week and stick to it.

Extend love and compassion toward yourself and others in community.

Share insights gleaned in silence with trusted spiritual companions. Be careful not to overexpose yourself. Sometimes people are not prepared to hear what you learn about God during silence.

Notice how the Holy Spirit moves in silence and in the rhythms of worship and other communal practices.

Practicing as a Spiritual Care Companion

Effective care emerges from our ability to sit in another's presence to see, feel, hear, and sense what is happening. Speaking follows whole body listening.

---

18. Margaret Guenther, *Holy Listening: The Art of Spiritual Direction* (Boston: Cowley, 1992), 44.

Healing and Wholeness

Contemplative practice energizes us toward freedom. We are like the person lying next to the pool of life for thirty-eight years, so close and yet so far from healing. Jesus asks: "Do you want to get well?" (John 5:6). Instead of saying yes, the man provides excuses: no one can lift him down, and others get in the way when the healing waters are stirred up (John 5:7). "Jesus said to him: 'Get up! Pick up your mat and walk'" (John 5:8). Like this man, we say, "I can't." Jesus's voice says, "Yes, you can." God sees our wellness and calls us to embrace it. Through contemplative spiritual practice, we get in touch with the body-inhibiting and body-limiting messages that keep us from dipping into the healing pool. Jesus's voice beckons: "Do you want to get well?" We are unsure because negative internalized messages block the way. Move through them and act now! Ease up on the resistances and let go of the negative messages and stories. Thirty-eight years is a long time to be unwell (John 5:5).

> **Question for Reflection:** What negative stories and resistances block your healing?

Silent Care

Silence can deepen presence with God and welcome us into "the family of things."[19] Silence can open us to the mystery and wonder of who we are and who God is, and it can pave the way for effective care. We often conceive of care as what we do *for* other people: shepherding, healing, guiding, empowering, and so on. But it is the *absence* of ego-filled doing that opens our capacity for *receiving* what God is already doing to help us receive our true identity. It is intimate work that requires quietly paying attention. Through non-doing or non-trying, we tap into the flow of care.[20] People might share emotionally difficult experiences with us. Tears or powerful feelings may erupt. We can receive and be with it all because

---

19. Mary Oliver, "Wild Geese," in *Dream Work* (New York: The Atlantic Monthly Press, 1986), 14.

20. See Siroj Sorajjakool, *The Practice of Wu-wei, Negativity, and Depression: The Principle of Non-Trying in the Practice of Pastoral Care* (Binghamton, NY: Haworth, 2001).

we are comfortable being with ourselves. We don't need to hide or run. We can be present in the bold silence.

A caring, silent presence calls for a kind of "undoing." We notice how we: encounter real social roadblocks, hold on to assumptions, and generate negative beliefs and story lines about self and others. We also notice how we: replay family-of-origin dynamics, get caught in emotional reactivity, and become absorbed in fantasies and preoccupations. We can participate in the undoing of these tendencies and patterns by seeing through the illusions and delusions that impede the embodiment of God's life and love within and around us.

Sitting with God in contemplative prayer can be anything but quiet. We become aware of the noise of thought. "Thought" names a broad array of mind processes that keep us from dwelling with God in the present and includes an idea, emotion, memory, inner dialogue, or preoccupation with a sense relating with body (such as a sound or an itch).[21] We catch ourselves absorbed in thought and focus instead on our breath, the sounds of nature, or a personally meaningful word such as *peace*. Otherwise, silent prayer becomes a reinforcement or tool of our ego. We find ourselves "thinking" instead of "praying," and there is a big difference. We return attention to the *imago Dei*, our essential relatedness to God experienced and sensed through our bodies.

Many types of thought can become distractions in silent prayer. They range from the benign to the more troublesome: (1) *mental loops* like making a grocery list, which are usually just a kind of spinning that the mind does before settling into silent prayer; (2) *attractive thoughts*, those with a positive emotional pull such as planning a vacation; (3) *repulsive thoughts*, those with a negative emotional tug such as a fight with a spouse; (4) *self-reflection* or a watching of the self in prayer; (5) *thoughts from the unconscious*, which is emotional pain that gives way to tears or an eruption of anger or anxiety.[22] As we practice in silence, we become familiar with our thought patterns! One teacher uses the phrase "frozen emotion thought"

---

21. Bourgeault, *Centering Prayer*, 36.
22. Bourgeault, *Centering Prayer*, 35–39.

to describe emotions and thoughts being tightly held in the body. As we rest into silent prayer, we can sense the thawing of the ice. We are released into God's flow of life.

> **Practice Point: Some Things Resolve Themselves**
>
> When we feel pressed and pressured our bodies show signs of stress. While it is not always a solution, stepping back and creating space can allow things to resolve themselves.
>
> What stress are you experiencing right now? How and where can you "step back"?

It is helpful not to judge the thoughts we encounter. Otherwise, prayer becomes punishment. We do need fortitude, though, as we come to see ourselves in all our "damaged glory."[23] Mostly we need to be prepared for what Thomas Keating, a teacher of centering prayer, calls "unloading the unconscious." This process includes "the spontaneous release of previously unconscious emotional material from early childhood in the form of primitive feelings or a barrage of images or commentaries."[24] For spiritual seekers intentional about their own psychological health and well-being, this process may be less intense because the inner landscape has been previously tended through pastoral counseling or psychotherapy. The release may still happen, but we are less inclined to be interrupted by the material. We simply make note of it for future reflection or a conversation with a trusted other, and return to silence. Contemplative practice and silent prayer work through our bodies and life experience like therapy. We come to see, to embrace, and to live from the true self and let go of or "dissolve" the false self.[25] We see and embrace our light and our shadow. We come to know that God holds us in love through it all.

---

23. The phrase comes from a collection of stories: Raphael Bob-Waksberg, *Some Who Will Love You in All Your Damaged Glory* (New York: Alfred A. Knopf, 2019).

24. Thomas Keating, *Foundations for Centering Prayer and the Christian Contemplative Life: Open Mind, Open Heart; Invitation to Love; The Mystery of Christ* (New York: Continuum, 2002), 250.

25. Thomas Keating, *Intimacy with God* (New York: Crossroad, 2009), 179.

Silent prayer opens the doorway to release the unconscious, but we do not need to be blown away. We gain traction by staying present with our bodies and pushing the "pause" button when surprising material surfaces. Consider the following options. **Practice by:** acknowledging the message; temporarily setting it aside for later consideration; asking, "what's this?" to invite more information; breathing with it; temporarily changing surroundings; or confronting it. Keep a pad handy to take notes for future processing by oneself or in conversation with a faith companion, trusted friend, spiritual director, or pastoral psychotherapist.

Silent Care: Breathing Practice

We tend to hold our breath or to take shallow breaths. Imagine slowly drawing breath into your lower abdomen, just below your belly button. Notice the difference in how this breathing practice releases tension and settles the body. Shallow breathing is like sipping air. It doesn't invigorate and energize the body.

We may take shallow breaths as a body defense, to avoid feeling the full force of emotions and life within us. A simple silent breathing practice is a care prayer. We quietly and attentively notice what is going on with the body. Breathing tunes us in and serves as body anchor for ourselves and others in our presence.

Practice: Draw your breath in slowly, filling the abdomen, and gently release. Repeat ten times. Note how you feel after doing so.

Reflect: Breath-awareness practice is rooted in the biblical tradition. Genesis 2:7: "Then the LORD God formed the human from the dust of the ground, and breathed into that one's nostrils the breath of life" (NRSV with my adjustments). *Nephesh* is the Hebrew word used for "breath" or "throat"; it comes to mean the whole person.

Engage: Breathing complements listening in spiritual care; it is a dual-focus exercise. Practice intentional breathing as you listen to another person. What do you notice?

Silent Care: Qigong Practice

Upon arriving to teach English in the People's Republic of China in the 1980s, I observed people in recreation fields, parks, and other community spaces engaged in *qigong*. The term means "cultivating of life energy" and is comprised of the Chinese word *qi*, life-energy, and *gong*, cultivation. The practice has a complex modern history.[26] Beginning practitioners can benefit in learning from teachers who know the practice well.[27]

Qigong is a term to describe body movement techniques that can be used as a form of exercise, martial art, or medicine.[28] Here qigong is introduced as a complement for spiritual practice and care. It is important to listen to the body in order to avoid injury. Consultation with a physician or other medical professional is advisable before beginning this or any other body practice. Simple body movement can put us in touch with the energy of life and God's healing Holy Spirit.

> **Practice:** Qi Walking cultivates awareness. We walk with the body in alignment by standing tall and lengthening the back, pointing feet forward, and engaging stomach muscles.
>
> **Reflect:** In Christian churches, people engage the ancient practice of walking a labyrinth as a means to encounter God's call in their lives. In Zen Buddhism, practitioners practice walking as "meditation off the cushion." Science reinforces the physical and psychological benefits of walking: "Our brain activity changes when we move about, with electrical brain rhythms that were previously quiescent now engaged and active."[29]
>
> **Engage:** Bring attention and focus to walking as a physical form of prayer and meditation. See what difference it makes in your daily life and connection to God and others.

---

26. To learn more about the development of *qigong* in China, see David A. Palmer, *Qigong Fever: Body, Science, and Utopia in China* (New York: Columbia University Press, 2007).

27. To learn more about qigong as a practice for healing, I recommend teachers, Dr. Eva Lew, MD and Master Frank Chan, and the resources available at http://www.medicinebeginswithme.com.

28. For a thorough resource on qigong and the practice of medicine, see *Energy Medicine East and West: A Natural History of QI*, eds. David Mayor and Marc S. Micozzi (London: Churchill Livingstone, 2011).

29. Shane O'Mara, *In Praise of Walking: A New Scientific Exploration* (New York: W. W. Norton, 2020), 7.

Chapter 6

Silence as Covenant Embodiment

In silent spiritual practice, we see God uncover all that hides our true face. We sense a change, and others see it. So it was with Moses in the descent from Mount Sinai: "As he came down from the mountain with the two covenant tablets in his hand, Moses didn't realize that the skin of his face shone brightly because he had been talking with God" (Exod 34:29). Upon seeing that Moses's face was shining, the people "were afraid to come near him" (Exod 34:30). Moses put on a veil as a buffer between him and the people, but he would take the veil off when "he went in to speak with the LORD" (Exod 34:35). Moses's face shines with reflected glory. When we come face-to-face with our God's deepest "yes" and our life purpose, our faces shine.

Contemplative practice and care put us in touch with God's covenant affirmation of "yes" to life. The prophet Micah offers a poetic encapsulation of embodying covenant: "With what should I approach the LORD and bow down before God on high?" (Mic 6:6). A litany of "nots" follow: *not* burnt offerings, *not* thousands of rams, *not* tens of thousands of rivers of oil, *not* my firstborn. All the "noes" keep us from embodying the "yeses" of covenant: "He has told you, human one, what is good and what the LORD requires from you: to do justice, embrace faithful love, and walk humbly with your God" (Mic 6:8). We move through a litany of "noes" and finally arrive at a body-resounding "yes," walking humbly with our God, face-to-face.

The book of Isaiah offers a poetic and searing reminder to the exiles of who they are:

> But now, says the LORD—the one who created you, Jacob, the who formed you, Israel: Don't fear, for I have redeemed you; I have called you by name; you are mine. When you pass through the waters, I will be with you; when through the rivers, they won't sweep over you. When you walk through the fire, you won't be scorched and flame won't burn you. I am the LORD your God, the holy one of Israel, your savior. I have given Egypt as your ransom, Cush and Seba in your place. Because you are precious in my eyes,

you are honored, and I love you. I give people in your place, and nations in exchange for your life. (Isa 43:1-4).

Worn down and weary from years in punishing exile, the people of Israel are comforted by the prophet's message. God reminds Israel of the actions taken on Israel's behalf. Covenant love is not hollow and divorced from reality. Covenant is grounded in God's history of acting toward Israel's well-being as a body of people. In care, we help people listen for and embody God's "I love you."

Similarly, Paul tells the community at Corinth that they are called to be ministers of the new covenant by reflecting the Spirit's glory by living in such a way that others can read their actions like a love letter from God. God is writing a letter *in us* for others to read. We encounter God's presence so that "all of us are looking with unveiled faces at the glory of the Lord as if we were looking in a mirror. We are being transformed into that same image from one degree of glory to the next degree of glory. This comes from the Lord, who is the Spirit" (2 Cor 3:18). Churches and other communities of care reflect God's glory as they come face-to-face with their identity and purpose.

In the Reformed tradition, churches baptize infants and through this practice communicate a profound theological message: God loves us before we can even choose to love. Baptism is a covenant practice with the body. At Jesus's baptism a voice comes from heaven, "You are my Son, the Beloved; with you I am well pleased" (Luke 3:21-22 NRSV). In baptism, we, too, receive bodily affirmation of being God's loved ones. It is the "I love you" resonance of baptism into which we re-immerse ourselves through contemplative, silent practice. We strip away the accumulated debris of persona,[30] false self system,[31] or "the whole 'me'-network"[32] to remember who and whose we are.

---

30. Carl Jung uses persona to refer to the face we show or mask we wear.

31. Ann Ulanov, *Religion and the Unconscious* (Philadelphia: Westminster, 1975), 19.

32. By this phrase, Toni Packer refers to all the conditioned patterns and thoughts generated by our minds that reinforce a sense of a separate self. See *The Silent Question: Meditating in the Stillness of Not-Knowing* (Boston: Shambhala, 2007), 162.

Chapter 6

Care ministers embody "yes" for people by listening and helping them discern through all the "noes" in their lives. Care providers communicate to people: you matter. Covenant wholeness recognizes humanity's "woundedness, but there is holiness as well."[33] Caregivers and care seekers together bring "gentleness, patience, consent, and a willingness to let the process . . . unfold."[34]

> **Questions:** Allow God's "I love you" to resonate in you. What do you notice in your body?
>
> When you bask in the experience of being loved, what aspects of your persona or false self system drop away? Do you sense yourself easing up on self-expectations such as "I should" or "I ought"? Reflect and share with others.

Keeping Covenant

The following steps can help you get started with silent prayer.[35] Clear physical space and create a sanctuary environment conducive to being still for a while. Choose to sit in a comfortable and upright position, preferably on a cushion or in a chair.

---

33. Bourgeault, *Centering Prayer*, 99.

34. Bourgeault, *Centering Prayer*, 99.

35. Gratitude is expressed to the Zen Center of San Diego for meditation teaching instructions that inform the practice outlined here.

1. Check your body.

   a. Sit in an upright but not uptight posture (no slouching or hunching over).

   b. Ease your facial expression and muscles.

   c. Soften any tension in your body.

2. Sit in silence. Focus on your breath, nature sounds, or a sacred word such as *peace*.

   When any thought comes into your head, gently

   Recognize it.

   Refrain from fueling it.

   Return to the breath, nature sound, or sacred word.

Here is another way to *think* about thoughts in centering (silent) prayer: resist no thought, retain no thought, react to no thought, and return to the sacred word.[36] A sacred word may be helpful; if so, choose a word or phrase that you can rest with and return to, such as *peace*, *love*, or *ruach*. The word helps you rest in God and is not meant to stimulate thoughts.

Duration: Try the practice above every day for ten minutes. Continue for one month. Increase the time by two minutes, and practice for twelve minutes every day for another month. Continue to increase the time by two minutes each month until you reach twenty minutes per day of silent prayer.

Choose a time of day and location that suit you (e.g., early morning on the chair in your den; or every evening on an enclosed patio). Stick with it.

---

36. Cynthia Bourgeault, *The Heart of Centering Prayer: Nondual Christianity in Theory and Practice* (Boston: Shambhala, 2016), 131.

Chapter 6

Elijah is a zealous prophet, actively engaged in doing God's work in the world, against the backdrop of leaders who do not keep God's covenant. Elijah's story testifies to the "power of God of Israel to work wonders grander than foreign gods and to provide for the people."[37] Possibly worn down and weary, God protects and provides for Elijah in the desert where he finds renewed purpose. Elijah stumbles into God's silence.

Here is the passage from 1 Kings 19: "[God said to Elijah], 'Go out and stand on the mountain before the Lord, for the Lord is about to pass by.' Now there was a great wind, so strong that it was splitting mountains and breaking rocks in pieces before the Lord, but the Lord was not in the wind; and after the wind an earthquake, but the Lord was not in the earthquake; and after the earthquake a fire, but the Lord was not in the fire; and after the fire a sound of sheer silence" (vv. 11-12 NRSV).

The 1 Kings passage offers practices for individuals and communities on a faith journey: (1) **Encountering fear** ("Then he was afraid; he got up and fled for his life" [1 Kings 19:3 NRSV]) and wanting a way out ("He asked that he might die" [1 Kings 19:4b]). We hide in our own real and imagined caves. Are they places of refuge or escape or both? (2) **Eating real food.** God in the form of an angel provides food ("Suddenly an angel touched him and said to him, 'Get up and eat.' He looked, and there at his head was a cake baked on hot stones, and a jar of water" [1 Kings 19:5b-6 NRSV]). Our bodies need actual sustenance to make the journey. (3) **Enduring the journey**. Elijah eats a second time ("He got up and ate and drank; then he went in the strength of that food forty days and forty nights to Horeb the mount of God" [1 Kings 19:8]). This shows Elijah needs feeding on two different levels. He needs both emotional and spiritual sustenance to nurture his body, mind, and spirit back to wholeness. (4) **Opening to silence**. Many movements precede Elijah's encounter with God in silence. He dismisses his servants and is alone "under a solitary broom tree," an image that reinforces his aloneness. He needs

---

[37]. Cameron B. R. Howard, "1 and 2 Kings," in *Women's Bible Commentary*, ed. Newsom, Ringe, and Lapsley, 172.

to prepare himself for encountering God in silence by separating himself from others. He initially flees for protection and discovers his call and purpose transformed as he attunes himself to God's vibrancy. Like Elijah, we discover God's presence in sheer silence.

Care ministries can be designed to meet different levels of needs. At the UCLA Medical Center, the chaplain's office used to host tea/coffee and cookie times in different units of the hospital. Staff would come for a brief respite from the demands of their work. Others came to share food together and get emotional and spiritual sustenance to continue their care. A few would come to sit for a while and listen to music on the tape player. Chaplains come prepared to engage with those who want to process anxieties, stresses, and struggles. For all, they created a space for gathering, sharing, and dropping into reflective silence.

Our ability to calm down and tune in to silence changes our bodies, as researcher Herbert Benson demonstrates.[38] His relaxation protocol can be helpful in halting or limiting stressors that cause disease in the body. Physicians are encouraged to use this technique alongside surgery and drug therapy to offer whole person treatment to patients. Ministers and lay people can adapt and incorporate this method in community and spiritual care settings. It can be used in workshops, retreats, church meetings, youth groups, Bible studies, interfaith conversations, and community engagement institutes, among others. It helps tune our bodies in to the healing nature of silence.

---

38. Herbert Benson is a Harvard physician and researcher who has devoted his entire career to study of mind-body healing. Relaxation changes the body's genetic activity. See Herbert Benson, MD and William Proctor, JD, *Relaxation Revolution* (New York: Scribner, 2011), 20–30.

Chapter 6

Relaxation Response[39]

Step 1: Pick a focus word, phrase, image, or short prayer. Or focus only on your breathing during this exercise.

Step 2: Find a quiet place and sit calmly in a comfortable position.

Step 3: Close your eyes.

Step 4: Progressively relax all your muscles.

Step 5: Breathe slowly and naturally. As you exhale, repeat or picture silently your focus word or phrase, or simply focus on your breathing rhythm.

Step 6: Assume a passive attitude. When other thoughts intrude, simply think, "Oh well," and return to your focus.[40]

Step 7: Continue with this exercise for an average of twelve to fifteen minutes.

Step 8: Practice this technique at least once daily.

Silent prayer opens the heart of compassion and connections within communities, as the following story suggests. During a period of quiet prayer in a room of twenty people, someone began to weep. At first only slight sounds of sniffling and breathing could be heard, and then the intensity increased. Crying echoed in the silence. Everybody sensed the experience of release. We are connected body-to-body with one another's suffering and joy. We might ordinarily wall ourselves off from the wounded pain-body,[41] but we might also try another way. We can create sanctuary by sitting quietly together in a candlelit room with steady, relaxed attention in breathing and listening. Silence heals. "We carry a lot of pain deep inside us, buried in our emotions and in our bodies."[42] Silence can also be a source of connection for people within and across denominations and faith traditions.

---

39. Taken from Benson and Proctor, *Relaxation Revolution*, 94–95.
40. I offer a revision of saying "not now" instead of "oh well."
41. Eckart Tolle. See *The Power of Now* (Novato, CA: New World, 2004).
42. Bourgeault, *Centering Prayer*, 39.

Body Care Prayer

God be in my head
And in my understanding.
God be in my mine eyes
And in my looking.
God be in my mouth
And in my speaking.
God be in my heart
And in my thinking,
God be at mine end
And at my departing.
—Sarum Primer, 1527[43]

This eleventh-century prayer expresses faithful desire: to embody God's presence in daily life. May it be so.

---

43. "Sarum Primer is a collection of prayers and worship resources developed in Salisbury, England during the thirteenth century. 'Sarum' is the abbreviation for the Latin word for Salisbury. The collection was used throughout Britain as well as parts of Continental Europe, until the Reformation." See the resources developed by the Unitarian Universalist Society: https://www.harvardsquarelibrary.org/poetry-prayers-visual-arts/sarum-primer, accessed June 1, 2021.

Chapter 7

GOD'S ARMOR AND OUR BODIES

Pastor John got word that a member of his community had been shot dead. The family was, of course, emotionally reeling from the news. This shooting followed closely on the heels of another recent death in the family. It seemed like too much to bear. The family and surrounding community was experiencing waves of shock and grief. The pastor arrived at the home and never got beyond the driveway. A family member of the deceased met him and said, "We don't need someone to say it's going to be all right." So, instead of offering words of false assurance and little comfort, Pastor John stood in the driveway and hugged. For five hours, he just hugged and cried with people.

The pastor's experience shared above captures the essence of "being there" for other in embodied care. The story also prompts questions. What does protection entail in a situation such as this? What resources and other support might be helpful for the surviving family members and neighbors? How can church leaders offer vital spiritual practices against the backdrop of trauma and violence? These questions inform reflection in this chapter.

Rabbi Hillel was a Jewish scholar who lived during Jesus's time. Hillel is widely known for the following quotation: "If I am not for myself, who will be for me? If I am only for myself, what am I?" This statement conveys complex and forthright wisdom for our time. The dominant popular culture message we hear is, "You have to look out for #1." The culture emphasizes self-absorbed individualism. But that is not what Rabbi Hillel urges. His message has covenant love at its heart: we need to care for ourselves because God has gifted us with life, and our bodies are vehicles of God's blessing and grace. But if we only look out for ourselves, we negate our God-inspired identity as beloved creatures of the Holy who cares for us and all of creation.

We explore spiritual care benefits of "putting on the armor of God." Protective spiritual practice is about honoring God and the gift of our bodies, so we can in turn offer care freely with others. We are self-attuned, but not self-preoccupied. This stance allows us to be adaptively present to what is needed in any given situation. Doing so allows us to be less guarded and more available to offer embodied care just as Pastor John was able to do. The armor of God also becomes a form of body protection for people who have experienced trauma and for those who are in difficult situations of grief and pain. Body armor helps people of faith show up with care and navigate the open and hidden wounds people bear.

Making Space Safe for Bodies

Trauma means "wounding" and is, unfortunately, all too prevalent. A concept of trauma is described as follows: individual trauma results from an event, series of events, or set of circumstances that is experienced by an individual as physically or emotionally harmful or life-threatening and that has lasting adverse effects on the individual's functioning and mental, physical, social, emotional, or spiritual well-being.[1] Trauma occurs in manifold ways through: intimidation, incest and rape, combat, domestic violence, car accidents, natural disasters, and gun and police violence, to name only a few. Racism, sexism, and other forms of systemic bias compound the experience of trauma for individuals and communities. It is most helpful to develop a trauma-informed approach to spiritual care.

Our role is to make our homes, churches, schools, and community centers safe spaces for all bodies by educating ourselves and others about the four Rs of trauma: (1) We *realize* that trauma can affect individuals,

---

1. "SAMHSA's Concept of Trauma and Guidance for a Trauma-Informed Approach" (October 2014), www.samhsa.gov, 9–10.

families, groups, churches, and communities. We realize that there may be more than meets the eye in behavior patterns (not functioning, acting out, reacting). We realize they may be coping strategies to deal with past or current trauma. We come to realize that these coping strategies may manifest in those who provide services to the traumatized. It is often referred to as secondary trauma. (2) We *recognize* the signs and symptoms of trauma. (3) We *respond* by establishing practices, procedures, and policies that protect the vulnerable from trauma. (4) We *resist* retraumatizing people by addressing issues that lead to stress and toxic environments.[2]

A trauma-informed approach is proactive and wide awake to reality and connected to the theology of covenant. Our "vertical" relationship with God calls us to a "horizontal" commitment to care for past, present, and future bodies. As trauma-informed people of faith, we pivot from "What's wrong with you?" to "What happened to you?"[3] We steer clear of harsh judgment and instead bring a compassionate mind-set to asking a caring question. We stay open as people share their stories. We might also allow for silence, since people may not be prepared to speak or may be unable to put words to their experience. Effective care providers endeavor to take measures to ensure the safety and well-being of all since bodies "hold the wreckage of traumatic experience(s)."[4]

Framing Care

As a professor of pastoral theology and care in a North American theological school, I regularly address the themes of self-care and spiritual practice in the classroom. Each class session begins with a modeling of self/spiritual care practice that opens the way for further exploration in any given class. In teaching at the seminary and preaching in local congregations, I always assume the presence of people who have been traumatized. This includes sexual and domestic violence, intimate partner violence, as

---

2. samhsa.gov.

3. "What Is Trauma-Informed Care?" accessed July 1, 2020, https://www.traumainformedcare.chcs.org/what-is-trauma-informed-care/.

4. Jennifer Baldwin, *Trauma-Sensitive Theology: Thinking Theologically in the Era of Trauma* (Eugene, OR: Cascade, 2018), 6.

well as social and family shaming. I do not assume that people will tell me directly about that trauma, though sometimes there is self-disclosure in confidential class papers. I honor the telling, but I do not intentionally prompt it. I never want people to be coerced into sharing. People talk when they feel secure. We can assume that some form of traumatic wounding lurks just beneath the surface in social environments including churches. We need to teach and practice ministry in recognition of this reality and encourage leaders and lay people to do so as well.

Protection is a proactive faith mind-set that values bodily integrity. The need is most acute for those who have been traumatized. That could be any of us. Van der Kolk's definition of trauma could not be more succinct and informs the discussion here: "an inescapably stressful event that overwhelms people's coping mechanisms."[5] Traumatic events, unfortunately, occur all too frequently. As Judith Herman recognizes, "Traumatic events are extraordinary, not because they occur rarely, but rather because they overwhelm the ordinary human adaptations to life."[6] Along with Carolyn Yoder, I assume "a traumatic reaction needs to be treated as valid, regardless of how the event that induced it appears to anyone else."[7] We take up proactive faith practices to honor bodies—our own as well as others'. We practice as if any*body* could be harmed and with the hope that no one will be.

Some are trained for doing therapeutic care with trauma survivors. We can all be prepared as spiritual seekers and caregivers to create space and establish practices that are empowering and supportive. It is helpful to bear in mind Judith Herman's three "stages of recovery": (1) establishment of safety, (2) remembrance and mourning, and (3) reconnection with ordinary life. We can always help to ensure safe contexts that do not retraumatize people (stage 1) and to connect with God and one another in ways that are helpful and meaningful (stage 3). However, people should

---

5. Deborah van Deusen Hunsinger, *Bearing the Unbearable: Trauma, Gospel, and Pastoral Care* (Grand Rapids: Eerdmans, 2015), 4.

6. Judith Herman, *Trauma and Recovery* (New York: Basic Books, 2015), 33.

7. van Deusen Hunsinger, *Bearing the Unbearable*, 5.

not be forced into sharing their stories and processing emotions (stage 2). In an attempt to be helpful, we can inadvertently do harm.[8]

Guidance for Care

Our bodies bear the marks of joy and pain, so we need to be sensitively aware in caring for others and ourselves. God intends well-being and wholeness for us and all of creation. If something makes us feel uncomfortable or unsafe, then we need to stop and pay attention. Do not push yourself or others. Honor the resistance. Give yourself and others permission not to engage or proceed. Stay connected with trusted people who can help interpret your experience. Care providers need to give clear guidance and model a gentle presence for spiritual care and practice with the body.

Beginning Practice Points

It is our birthright as God's beloved creatures to advocate for self and others. Use the following statements as beginning reflection points to cultivate the habit of speaking up for justice.

- We do not let others silence our voice. Recognize that a situation may not allow for speaking out directly. However, this reality need not mean we shut down inwardly. Honor your own strength and hold on to your confidence.

- We step carefully through the thicket of dynamics in our families, churches, and organizations. We are not naively carried away by an ideal of how it "should be," but we stay grounded and work toward change with "what is."

We engage in practices of faith to know and love God more deeply and to live in right relationship with other people. But this is not easy to do in practice. Some of our relationships and situations in churches and

---
8. Herman, *Trauma and Recovery*.

at work come fraught with unwelcome dynamics. We develop bonds with others who challenge us and help us grow. We learn in relationships how to give of ourselves and to receive genuinely from others. We also need to be protected in order to prevent emotional, physical, psychological, or spiritual injury or to lessen the damage from injuries that have already occurred. People of faith, most especially those who have or will experience trauma, need safeguards in place. A protective stance honors us as God's beloved and establishes a boundary of self-regard and self-respect.

The Whole Armor of God

Here in its entirety is the passage on the whole armor of God from Ephesians 6:10-20 (NRSV):

> Finally, be strong in the Lord and in the strength of his power. Put on the whole armor of God, so that you may be able to stand against the wiles of the devil. For our struggle is not against enemies of blood and flesh, but against the rulers, against the authorities, against the cosmic powers of this present darkness, against the spiritual forces of evil in the heavenly places. Therefore take up the whole armor of God, so that you may be able to withstand on that evil day, and having done everything, to stand firm. Stand therefore, and fasten the belt of truth around your waist, and put on the breastplate of righteousness. As shoes for your feet put on whatever will make you ready to proclaim the gospel of peace. With all of these, take the shield of faith, with which you will be able to quench all the flaming arrows of the evil one. Take the helmet of salvation, and the sword of the Spirit, which is the word of God.
>
> Pray in the Spirit at all times in every prayer and supplication. To that end keep alert and always persevere in supplication for all the saints. Pray also for me, so that when I speak, a message may be given to me to make known with boldness the mystery of the gospel, for which I am an ambassador in chains. Pray that I may declare it boldly, as I must speak.

In its original context, this letter was addressed to a mixed audience that included freeborn and slave women and men.[9] In our time, the let-

---

9. See Elisabeth Schussler Fiorenza, *Ephesians*, Wisdom Commentary, vol. 50, ed. Linda M. Maloney and Barbara E. Reid (Collegeville, MN: Liturgical Press, 2017), xlviii. Schussler Fiorenza keeps gender

ter addresses similarly diverse audiences and communities with people of varying degrees of power and status. We interpret the metaphor through the lens of life experience. The passage can be used to champion imperialism and triumphalism. We do this by asserting Christian superiority and fighting the Christian fight against a world we imagine is hostile to its message. It can be used as a source to fuel the battle with spiritual forces "out there" in an abstract realm.

As the care scenarios below illustrate, we reckon with real forces in daily interactions in workplaces, churches, and schools. We encounter the forces "right here" in the fraught and frayed dynamics, and the body carries marks and memories of this trauma. I stand with those who have been or could be harmed and wounded and read this complex passage as a liberating message to address oppressive practices and structures. We need to read this scripture with a "hermeneutics of suspicion"[10] or "reading against the grain," that is, with the aim of opening new possibilities for faith and practices. We do well to question and wonder how this energizing metaphor can be gospel, or good news, for bodies under assault.

Power dynamics exist everywhere. We live in a web of relationships and within systems that hopefully foster well-being instead of "domination and exploitation."[11] As spiritual seekers and caregivers, we need to be alert to dominating and exploitive dynamics and work against them. This requires intentional effort, since we are imbedded in families and systems, and our ability to exercise power in any given environment is also influenced by social factors that define and limit us.

Sometimes our initial inclination is to dismiss the possibility that harmful dynamics could exist in a community with which we are associ-

---

and power analysis at the forefront of her interpretation. She uses "wo/men" to "to signify that there is no unified essence share by all wo/men . . . the category of 'woman' is already fractured and inflected by other structures of oppression." Further, "wo/men are not just defined by gender but also by race, class, ethnicity, age, and other social-political identity markers."

10. Schussler Fiorenza, *Ephesians*, Wisdom Commentary, xlviii.

11. Elisabeth Schussler Fiorenza uses "*kyriarchy/kyriocentrism*, derived from the Greek *kyrios* (emperor, lord, master, father, husband) in order to specify that in Western societies the system of domination and exploitation is not just patriarchal but *kyriarchal*—that is, it is defined not just by gender [but] also by race, class, ethnicity, imperialism, and age." *Ephesians*, Wisdom Commentary, xlviii.

ated. We need to practice wisdom as spiritual practitioners and recognize they could exist. We also would be well-served to consider that when one "hits a brick wall" or "bumps into a glass ceiling" or "gets a cold shoulder," these matters are not all just in our heads. Our bodies are encountering something real. Relational and institutional dynamics are at work. Even as we commit ourselves to using power wisely so that it enlarges justice for all, we should not assume this is necessarily the case for everyone around us.

Ephesians offers a way through circumstances for those who have their senses open and know the world is not always a friendly place. It does not offer a call for revolutionary change in social structures and power dynamics. The passage and practices it suggests offer a way to live with integrity and faith through challenging circumstances. It is a message for people who live in the real world. To those who have been wounded and traumatized: here is a means to protect yourself. Ephesians does not "change the kyriarhcial status system of Greco-Roman society but reinscribes it in terms of the status and values of the Roman Empire."[12] Sometimes all the traumatized can muster is not to become harmed again. Justice may eventually come for those who have been injured and harmed through words and deeds. But they/we might have to wait a long time. What is needed now is safety. Clinicians who care for individuals and communities who have been traumatized remind us that seeking safety is the first priority. If we do not feel safe, then we certainly cannot grow and thrive. Putting on the whole armor of God is the protective gear we need. It offers a safety bubble to engage in the world as we know and encounter it.

> **Protective Body Practices:** Bring to mind a time when you were caught off guard and did not feel emotionally safe. What protective gear would have been most helpful?
>
> How can God's armor provide internal body strength for troublesome situations you encounter?

---

12. Schussler Fiorenza, *Ephesians*, Wisdom Commentary, lxxx.

As children, we learn to build another kind of body armor that protects us from emotions that others do not want us to express. Wilhem Reich, a contemporary of Sigmund Freud, coined the term *character armor* to describe "the physical manifestation of psychological protection from childhood wounds."[13] As children, we learn to protect ourselves from undesirable emotions by holding the tension within the muscles in our bodies. Instead of expressing anger or rage, for example, which would probably not be well-received by adults, we might contract muscles in the chest or stomach in order to suppress emotion. How and where we hold emotions in our bodies differs for each one of us. Character armor is an unconscious form of protection that helps us navigate our surroundings. A coping mechanism helpful in childhood, though, causes problems in adulthood as we hold back unwelcome emotions and restrict access to living fully and expressively.

Breath work and other body-oriented practices aid the ability to release the character armor restrictions. Such practices complement talking with a therapist who can help people work through life challenges and conflicts. Today, clinicians and theorists propose that body-oriented therapies serve a key function in healing through trauma.[14] As ministers and care seekers, most of us will develop an eclectic approach to health and well-being. We use what works and take caution to do no harm to others or ourselves.

---

13. Vincentia Schroeter, "Character Armoring: A Wall Between Oneself and the World," in *The Revelation of the Breath: A Tribute to Its Wisdom, Power, and Beauty*, ed. Sharon G. Mijares (Albany, NY: SUNY Press, 2015), 75.

14. Bessel van der Kolk, *The Body Keeps the Score: Brain, Mind, and Body in the Healing of Trauma* (New York: Penguin, 2014), 254–55.

Chapter 7

> **Body Focus**
>
> Restricted breathing causes tension to build up in the body. Notice what happens in your body as you move through the following steps:
>
> 1. Lift shoulders up into neck and roll shoulders forward.
>
> 2. Pull arms tightly into sides.
>
> 3. Pull in belly and tighten your waist.
>
> 4. Now, inhale and exhale.
>
> 5. Notice any constraints.[15]
>
> Here's my suggestion: use whatever practice seems helpful to take more life/breath into your body. Consider setting an alarm to breathe intentionally for two minutes every day. Gradually, lengthen the time if it is helpful. Take care not to do anything that would heighten anxiety or stress. Do what is right for you.

Protective Care

Interpersonal relationships can be wounding, so we need to take proactive steps to lessen the occurrences. We will look at the need for a protective care stance and practices with leadership in the workplace, in churches, and in neighborhoods. The insights and lessons from these scenarios intersect and provide springboards for reflection and practice in other contexts.

Workplace Hostility

I asked for a class volunteer to engage in a role play so I could demonstrate listening skills. Rachel, a sixty-year-old second-career student, quickly offered to participate. She readily shared real-life pain she endured while working at a federal agency. Highly competent, articulate, and organized, she described the stress of the heavy workload and how she adeptly

---

15. Exercise taken from Vincentia Schroeter, "Character Armoring: A Wall Between Oneself and the World," 80.

navigated the bureaucracy to develop policies helpful for people. While exhausted from the intensity and pace of the job, she also expressed satisfaction and conveyed pride in her accomplishments. Rachel narrowed in on the "hostile negativity" of the place. Several key leaders seemed intent on attacking people personally.

As she told her story, I sensed an immense well of pain in her, connected and yet deeper than the sum of all elements she was describing. As is often the case, we are not wounded by one thing, but by many. Trauma does not live by itself; it invites visitors. I sensed this was the case for Rachel as she wondered aloud through her tears whether she was "too broken" to be a minister. Though she strongly advocated for others, Rachel had trouble speaking up for herself. She pondered how to address the abusers in her former workplace. Whether in person or through a letter, she wanted to let them know how they were damaging people. Rachel desired to balance the scales of justice. Yet, as I listened with compassion, I sensed her inclination to enter this fraught environment with a kind and open heart seemed potentially harmful. I imagined her intention and action would expose her to wounding and would hook memories of other traumatic experiences.

She wanted to leverage her authority and power to prevent harm to others. I thought doing so would harm her. So I said, "How about protecting yourself by putting on the whole armor of God? Imagine a shield around you as protection from harm." As a man listening with a woman, I was conscious to avoid being or sounding paternalistic. I did not speak this message because I pitied Rachel or thought her to be incapable in any way. Rather, I was building an alliance with her strong inner self that I sensed was ready but hesitant to claim protection.

For Rachel, the words of empowerment initially puzzled her. As a woman, she learned and had reinforced through decades of experience that her role was to offer care and compassion to others. "I have a hard time caring for myself," Rachel acknowledged. In the class debriefing, another student commented: "You listened intently. When you suggested she protect herself, you did so in alliance with her. You were not giving advice. You were reminding her of another way." It was evocative learning for everyone.

> **Body Practices:** Consider your hesitancy to put your own integrity and well-being at the center instead of on the sidelines. What steps can you take to make a shift from hesitancy to strength?
>
> How and in what contexts do you need to give yourself permission to claim protection? What do you need to "unlearn"? What kinds of personal and community support would reinforce this practice?
>
> How does it feel in your body when others cast blame? Or when they offer refuge?

Bad Energy in the Community

A pastoral leader shared her story in a class discussion. Christine serves as an intentional interim minister for designated periods of time ranging from one to two years. She provides leadership in communities that need to re-establish administrative structures and cultivate relationships; sometimes communities are in need of healing from trauma or clergy sexual misconduct. Christine talked about the "bad energy" in one congregation. "They talked a nice game," she admitted, but "the vibe in the place was really off. People are not all right. They can be kind of shadowy." What might be called "church drama" has its roots in personal/communal trauma. People have been wounded and in turn wound others. It is no accident the interim pastor exclaims: "the powers of destruction are real." Traumatic wounds are at the core, and a lack of awareness leads people to tear themselves and others apart.

After a period of intense discussion, I urged: "You have to walk into a community like that with your armor on!" I could sense in my body the need for this pastoral leader to protect herself from the "bad energy." Protection is not an abstract idea but a real need.

> **Body Practice Questions:** How does your body signal the presence of "bad energy" in an environment or among a group of people? Do you heed the warning? How so? Or what keeps you from naming the reality when you sense it?
>
> Have you experienced circumstances in your personal life or in your community in which taking up the armor in advance was helpful or might have been helpful? Describe how so.
>
> Does thoughtful reflection lead to new body habits, or do you stay locked in your head? Identify what is needed to develop accountability and support for taking a step into actual practice.

Childhood Bullying

We need to protect ourselves from people who not only hold hostile views but also engage in harmful action. Timothy was traumatized in early adolescence by a group of kids who threatened to beat him up because his parents were a lesbian couple. He was viewed as different and subjected to bullying because the kids in his school internalized the biases and negative stereotypes they learned at home. After Timothy revealed the bullies' names to a school counselor, confidentiality was broken and news quickly spread in the community. People turned against the family. They blamed and shamed them out of town. The stress eventually led to his parents' separation.

Timothy drew a direct line between himself and this traumatic event. He took responsibility for the incidents perpetrated against him as well as the breaking apart of his family. He burrowed into a hole of self-blame, gloom, and guilt. In the following years, depressive episodes erupted intermittently and took over his life. At a low point when Timothy planned to take his own life, the metaphor of Ephesians provided spiritual therapy. "When the forces were coming at me, I imagined them clinking off the armor. So, these are not just words to me." God's word provided body armor.

Chapter 7

> **Body Practice:** Develop a prayer mantra (repetitive phrase) that resonates positively with your body. Try different words to see what works for you: "I am not to blame." "It's not my fault." "I cannot hold this alone."
>
> Beware of herd mentality and bystander syndrome. They both keep us from taking necessary action on behalf of someone being bullied and harmed. Anticipate in advance how you can resist the temptation to "go with the flow," which really means to do nothing.

Permeable Care

Protective spiritual practice enables healing from personal and social wounds that often blur together to cause ongoing pain. We do well to grow our faith and heal our bodies within churches that are committed to safe sanctuaries. Such covenant care communities engage in respectful patterns of relationship and communication while they also interrupt social patterns of abuse and violence that destroy lives. Protective spiritual practices and community together form what I call a "permeable spiritual security bubble." It keeps body and soul from injury and shields already existing wounds so that we can engage as whole people of faith in the world.

"Take it up, so you can withstand." This is an encouraging word for living in contexts of trauma. But the power of the passage does not stop there. I have students who describe the "prayer warriors" in their congregations. They are the ones who "do battle" with all that seeks to destroy body, mind, and spirit. "Prayer warrior" is an apt description for people who diligently urge God to deliver healing and protection. The armor metaphor also energizes "The Battle Hymn of the Republic," a still popular tune that conveys a triumphal message. The hymn casts a vision of a warrior God who uses a "terrible swift sword" and "marches on." This is an unfortunate and harmful rendering of the metaphor that valorizes God and people who celebrate conquest. It transforms the tools of spiritual and body protection into instruments of war.

We do not engage in protective practices because we harbor the notion that the world is out to get us. That mind-set comes from a defensive posture fueled by simmering grievances and inner wounds that lead to unhealthy aggressive actions. Protective spiritual practices fortify us to meet directly whatever we face in life. Self-care is step one for protection. That bears repeating until it becomes second nature for us. This step moves "against the grain" for spiritual seekers and caregivers who believe the concerns of others must come first. Our misguided view causes emotional, spiritual, and physical depletion that renders us unable to care for others. When we engage protective practices first, we signal to God and ourselves the desire to use wisely our bodies' vital energy. We are then better prepared to relate with people who have experienced trauma. We are also aware of the need to tend our own wounds that surface in care. Traumatic experience fragments us. Protective spiritual practice mends and tends.

"Protective" is a way to describe safeguarding our bodies through any religious or spiritual practice we engage. We do not hunker down and build walls, but we do engage in practice knowing that the forces we contend with in ourselves and in the world can be formidable. We commit ourselves to practice consistently and wisely in order to strengthen our bodies and minds just as an Olympic athlete would do. Through consistent practice over years, we come to see something of the spiral nature of reality and ourselves. It may seem as if we keep encountering the same struggles over and over again: work problems, relationship issues, difficult emotions, or whatever we wrestle with. Each moment is new, though, and we change as does our relationship with God and one another. There may be a familiar quality to the joys and challenges we encounter, but there are also differences and nuances. The spiral captures the felt sense of being able to see and experience simultaneously our inner and outer worlds as well as our depths and heights. God's presence relates to us wherever we are. Protective practices offer the support needed to heal and grow through the pains and wounds of life.

Chapter 7

Spiritual Practice: Taking Up Love and Getting Out of the Way

Years ago, a social worker colleague gave me wise two-fold advice for care: "love the beings" and "get out of the way." Love one another echoes from the New Testament letter, and we wonder: how? Getting out of the way names our ability to be present to ourselves and one another without interference. Love requires action to give it substance. To love other people in care requires: attention, body presence, open perspective, and tolerance for a wide range of thoughts and feelings. In care, we listen, ask clarifying questions, validate feelings, interpret and frame experience, and consider next steps. Love calls us to respond to the integrity and worth of the embodied persons in our presence. This calls for more than a clinical or professional demeanor. We encounter others as loved and whole creations of God.

Practices for Loving the Body-Self

Accepting the body as it is

Being in the present moment

Letting go of trying to control

Seeing through obsessive and circular thoughts

Getting sufficient sleep and regular exercise

"Getting out of the way" names the Other-centered or God-centered nature of ministry. It's about not needing to be someone important in the relationship; it's about allowing others to grow and learn about themselves as embodied persons. It's about being comfortable being with silence and saying nothing. It requires us to suspend being smart or witty or helpful. Getting out of the way in body care is at once being fully present with another person or within a group and allowing the Spirit to be the center of attention. Our ideas and perspectives can be most helpful when they relate with processes that are already underway in the body. But if we do not hold them lightly, our thoughts and suggestions can become burdensome weight for other people. At its best, getting out of the way is "being present" without drawing attention to ourselves. We give our attention to the unfolding inner experience of others.

> **Practices for Getting Out of the Way**
>
> Pausing for significant comments
>
> Allowing emotions to emerge
>
> Affirming whatever is present
>
> Giving attention to the other
>
> Not overstaying our welcome

Body Care Prayer

O Protective One,
You alone are the source of true power and strength. You create galaxies and spin planets. You form the earth and all its creatures. You energize our bodies for caring service in a world rife with misused power that traumatizes people and devastates communities. Give us the wisdom to take up protective practices as we forge a path of healing and peace for ourselves and in relationships with others. Enfold us with your fierce love so that we might release our minds from fear and open our hearts for caring compassion wherever our journey leads us.
Amen.

Chapter 8

HUMANIZING BODIES: EXPOSING AND TRANSFORMING STORIES

I was standing in a hotel lobby when I learned the news: Rev. Clementa Pinkney was shot and killed while leading a Bible study at Mother Immanuel Church in Charleston, South Carolina. He was a Doctor of Ministry student in a class I taught. A few hours after learning the news, I led an opening prayer at a professional meeting in which I named white violence against black bodies. I prayed through tears because I could not hold them back. A colleague later said, "You shared your vulnerability with us, and that is very meaningful." My body would not have allowed me to do otherwise.

Forensics classes teach that "silence is consent in debate." Each side must argue points and question assumptions in order to persuade the judges. The phrase applies to oppressive social patterns. If we do not speak up, our silence endorses things as they are. A student puts it this way: silence can be a bridge. It can also be a form of control. Silence is a form of control when it is held negatively: when we don't say or do something because we sense internal hesitation or group pressure. "The shame and anxiety about issues of orientation, sexuality, race, gender, and other aspects of our identities are difficult for many pastoral leaders to confront and often cause them to move away from conflict rather than engage differences of understandings and perceptions."[1] We expose negative silence individually and together as we publicly identify shame-based histories, relational dynamics, and secrets that subjugate bodies.

Social Secrets: Exposing Negative Silence and Shifting Language

We ought not to tiptoe around social dynamics that render people's bodies as less than fully human. Secrets and negative silence shame the body, make people feel less than whole, and tear apart communities. As spiritual seekers and communities of care, we create space for peeling back the layers of negative shame that tarnish the image of God and disregard humanity dignity.[2] This requires personal and collective effort. Each one of us has a part to play in telling stories of truth that contribute to the justice and well-being of human persons and God's creation. Belief structures or ideologies keep bodies locked in place. This works for the bodies who stand to benefit. Everybody else loses. White supremacy as an ideology "thwart[s] both the Christian gospel message and democratic ideals."[3] The term "white supremacy" describes the pervasive nature of interlinking social oppression that occurs through complex interactions of attitudes, decisions, habits, histories, and strategies. Furthermore, intersecting oppressions of sexism, classism, heterosexism, and ableism all distort human dignity. We start where we are—in our church, family, or place of work—to make changes to counter social patterns and policies that contribute to oppression and communicate negative body messages.

We help make change, in part, by resisting overt and exposing covert forms of white supremacy/racism. Overt forms include KKK demonstrations and the killing of Black, Brown, and Asian bodies. Covert forms,

---

[1]. Karla J. Cooper and Joretta L. Marshall, "Where Race, Gender, and Orientation Meet," in *Women Out of Order: Risking Change and Creating Care in a Multicultural World*, ed. Jeanne Stevenson-Moessner and Teresa Snorton (Minneapolis: Fortress, 2009), 121.

[2]. See Beverly Eileen Mitchell, *Black Abolitionism: A Quest for Human Dignity* (Maryknoll, NY: Orbis, 2005). Dr. Mitchell draws theological connections between human dignity and the *imago Dei* (pp. 4–7).

[3]. Mitchell, *Black Abolitionism*, 2.

among many possibilities, include policies, attitudes, and biases that undergird overt forms. Oppressive language about bodies comes in both overt and covert forms. A "whites-only drinking fountain" and derogatory racial slurs are examples of overt white supremacy.[4] Covert or "implicit racism" is coded in everyday language many use without realizing it. Scholars note that "master" and "slave" language—as in "master bedroom" and "master key"—shows vestiges of the nation's history of enslaving African people.[5] Knowledge is power. Once we become aware, hearing implicit racism used in language makes the body cringe. We revise our language as reflection of a commitment to justice for all bodies. We are not trying to be politically correct, as some would assert. Rather, we revise language as a moral action in service to dismantling the practices and policies that undergird overt forms of oppression.

We likewise can be mindful of language use related to human dignity and mental illness and dis/ability. The phrase "commit suicide," for instances, makes self-killing sound like a crime. Language encodes moral judgment, as in "suicide is unethical because God alone gives life." Consider using instead the phrase "death by suicide" or "took their own life." Scripture also encodes potentially harmful language if the metaphors are not adequately interpreted. Observe what Isaiah 42:18 says: "Hear, deaf ones, and blind ones, look and see!" This prophetic hymn of praise uses body descriptions of "deaf" and "blind" to reference all of God's people who have the capacity to hear and to see. We need to avoid using such language to marginalize and disempower people with dis/abilities.[6]

Our daily interactions provide opportunity to learn about and expose *oppressive body stories and experiences.* The stories depict interactions that bring to the surface dynamics and issues for reflection and action. Lived experience is, of course, complex and multilayered. Use these story vignettes to spark conversation in groups as you engage empathically around intersecting oppressions and their effects on your life. In regard to

---

4. "The Language of Racism: Why It's Time to Get Rid of Master Bedroom, Cake Walk, Grandfather Clause," *Here & Now*, National Public Radio, WBUR Boston, July 23, 2020.

5. See "The Language of Racism."

6. For a detailed examination on the topic of the Bible and dis/abilities, see Amos Yong, *The Bible, Disability, and the Church: A New Vision of the People of God* (Grand Rapids: Eerdmans, 2011).

Chapter 8

race: An African American colleague and I worked together on a teaching project. When we discussed self-introductions, my colleague said, "I want to be introduced as Dr. Washington." I usually give my first and last name and then say, "Please feel free to call me Michael." The self-introductions reflect different styles embedded in systems of cultural privilege. That immediately raised a question for me. It seemed awkward *to think about* using a title in addressing my colleague in front of the class. I pondered the matter and decided to do just that. I recognize and reinforce the privilege due my colleague in the academy and the church. For my part, I could give away privilege because as a white male I have already been assumed to have it. In the end, we acknowledged to each other how our teamwork flowed seamlessly. I wonder how the students felt about it. *Here's a helpful tip:* discuss titles and how you want to be addressed; allow for differences.

In regard to **gender:** A colleague and I were team teaching an advanced course in our field. She and I developed a plan that included detailed notes for leading and following up with seminar discussions. The plan established equity on paper. However, during one lively class session, I allowed discussion to extend beyond our agreed-upon time limit. This caused a problem. We had a moment of conflict as I stepped over my allotted time frame. As a woman, my colleague had previously experienced many occasions of being sidelined. This situation prompted body memory of all the other times. I listened to her frustration and apologized. I acknowledge how my embodiment as a white male and all the privileges that come with it plays a role in circumstances whether or not I intend it. *Here's a helpful tip:* face and talk about missteps; do not cover them over.

In regard to **class:** A former parishioner, who is a brilliant woman who grew up poor in upstate New York, tells of the shame exposed in learning about class distinctions. "People notice class. They just don't talk it," she sighed in resignation. A high-school guidance counselor advised her not to apply to Ivy League schools for college. "You wouldn't fit in. There would be too much of a gap." She, of course, knew what the counselor meant. The advice came with a heavy dose of classism. "Wouldn't fit in" is code language for money as well as social distinctions. You wouldn't be able to afford to fit in. You wouldn't have the right sensibilities to fit in.

This is an alienating message for anyone to internalize, and especially an intellectually gifted teenager. *Here's a helpful tip* for those with privilege: check your language for embedded assumptions about class.

> **Titles and Respect: Gender, Race, and Class**
>
> **Individual and Group Reflection Questions:** What titles of respect do you expect others to use in referencing you? Do you use titles in referencing others? Why or why not? How do you think these social protocols are related to gender, race, and class?
>
> **It's Not Selfish**
>
> In worship one Sunday during the pandemic, an African American gentleman in a multiethnic congregation prefaced his prayer request by saying, "This may be selfish, but I want to pray for all teachers and their anxiety about going back to school." It was a heart-filled statement. I could not let the assumption beneath the statement go unchallenged. "Praying for a way through our own anxiety is not being selfish." We sometimes need others to give us permission to make our bodies' safety a priority. Over time, we can internalize this empowering practice for ourselves.
>
> In circumstances in which you put yourself down or prioritize others' needs above your own, practice stating silently or aloud, "Not selfish. Not selfish. Not selfish," before you make the request known.

Ibrahim X. Kendi argues, "Race is a mirage but one that humanity has organized itself around in very real ways."[7] The word mirage captures my attention and calls to mind The Four Bodhisattva Vows, a familiar chant in Zen Buddhism. The Upaya Zen Center in Sante Fe, New Mexico, uses the following version:[8]

Creations are numberless, I vow to free them.
Delusions are inexhaustible, I vow to transform them.
Reality is boundless, I vow to perceive it.
The awakened way is unsurpassable, I vow to embody it.

---

7. Ibrahim X. Kendi, *How to Become an Antiracist* (London: Oneworld, 2019), 108.

8. "The Four Great Bodhisattva Vows," Upaya Institute and Zen Center, https://upaya.org/teachings/liturgy/four-great-bodhisattva-vows, accessed August 4, 2020.

The second vow, "Delusions are inexhaustible, I vow to transform them," names a wholehearted commitment to see through delusions and mirages as a step toward humanizing bodies. Racism is a mirage and delusion that creates separation and causes suffering for countless bodies. Delusions distort reality and infect everything they touch. Racism, white supremacy, and every other ideology that attempts to render bodies as "less human" are burdensome and oppressive mirages. A colleague once said about combating racism: "it is exhausting." I hear the lament. May each community and person choose to take up a piece of racial justice advocacy in service to human dignity and the restoration and well-being of the whole body.

We cut through delusions just as we also expose secrets and transform negative silences in order to become more fully human. As spiritual practitioners, we realize our being is bound in covenant loyalty with other bodies, including those of previous and future generations. Delusions get reinforced when we say to ourselves: "I am not that." One possible "delusion" white people hold with regard to racism is thinking, "I am not racist." We can miss seeing how our interaction within systems perpetuates the problem. "Racism is a marriage of racist policies and racist ideas that produces and normalizes racial inequities."[9] Owning the problem is one way of doing something about it. Racist ideas and policies need to be transformed. "An anti-racist policy is any measure that produces or sustains racial inequity between racial groups" and includes "written and unwritten laws, rules, procedures, processes, regulations, guidelines that govern people."[10] Spiritual seekers and communities make a vow to develop such policies as part of the larger project to embody practices that recognize humanity dignity.

Through humanizing body practices, we contribute to the work of justice. We *develop resistance* to creating negative silence and perpetuating harmful secret keeping. We develop resistance to mind-sets that render any person as a second-class person and keep them oppressed. Paulo Freire argues that the oppressed themselves need to develop a critical con-

---

9. Kendi, *How to Become an Antiracist*, 38.
10. Kendi, *How to Become an Antiracist*, 38.

sciousness in order to resist dominant ideologies from taking root in the mind.[11] To acquiesce to and accommodate harmful situations allows them to continue. But it is also risky for individual persons/bodies to make changes, given the tenacity of interlocking systems of power that perpetuate structures of oppression. We *build connections* through social solidarity. One manifestation of this commitment has been the display of "Black Lives Matter" signs placed prominently in private and public spaces. They appear in home and store windows and on walls and on streets in the wake of George Floyd's murder in May 2020. The phrase "I can't breathe" has become a rallying cry for reform of unjust systems and practices. For many, social solidarity emerges from experiencing "grief born of injustice," which is "caused by unjust structures and/or by unjust actions or inactions of individuals, groups, and systems."[12] This is grief following that which never should have happened. Our bodies take to the streets to voice anger and rage at the injustice. Grief needs to take action.

As spiritual practitioners and communities we start somewhere with humanizing body practices, and we stay open to learning through the process. One congregation determined to address its own white racism decided to partner with a local school to tutor children. The group pushed for action because they were anxious to offer a quick fix, prompted by their own sense of guilt. The group wanted to avoid sitting with body discomfort. This practice of being with our bodies is just what is needed, though, to allow authentic transformation to unfold from the inside out. We stay in touch with our bodies to hear the body needs of others. We refrain from imposing our experience and ideas on others. We do commit, though, to being changed as we vow to make change.

Shameful Secrets

Emma Justes defines "shameful secrets" as circumstances "kept hidden or unexplained, out of public view, and permeated with shame. Shameful

---

11. See Paulo Freire, *Pedagogy of the Oppressed*, 4th ed. (London: Bloomsbury Academic, 2018).

12. Melissa M. Kelly, *Grief: Contemporary Theory in the Practice of Ministry* (Minneapolis: Fortress, 2010), 15.

secrets may be kept for long periods of time, even for generations. Secret keepers fear exposure, and sometimes the secrets are kept even from the conscious self."[13] We probably know either from our own or other's experience the damage done by keeping shameful secrets in personal and family relationships. What we may not recognize is that keeping shameful secrets also has a social dimension. Secret keeping within churches, schools, and other organizations creates system imbalances and erodes patterns of equity, justice, and inclusion. Some might say: "Well, if it does not personally affect me, there is no problem." As people committed to the awakening journey in our bodies, though, we ought not to become complicit in shame-filled secret keeping and perpetuation at any level. We seek, instead, to expose secrets and practice care.

Here's the problem: secrets fuel social pacts and influence behavior that creates "insiders" and "outsiders." This division blocks the vitality of the whole body and is experienced most keenly by those left out. The reverberations of keeping secrets and maintaining divisions carry throughout a lifetime and across generations. Secrets do harm by breaking covenant to love God, ourselves, and one another. Exodus 34:6-7 captures God's voice in the matter: "The LORD passed in front of him and proclaimed: 'The LORD! The LORD! a God who is compassionate and merciful, very patient, full of great loyalty and faithfulness, showing great loyalty to a thousand generations, forgiving every kind of sin and rebellion, yet by no means clearing the guilty, punishing for their parents' sins their children and their grandchildren, as well as the third and the fourth generation.'" God embodies steadfast commitment and serves warning about breaking covenant; acts have consequences, and the ripple effects extend for generations. Let us instead choose to become keepers of the covenant and stewards of justice in the transformation of shame-filled stories for the sake of our own and others' bodies.

Exposing secrets and negative silences can be messy and confusing because of the emotions that emerge. We might grieve and celebrate, feel sadness and relief. Sharing secrets changes our lives, and we are not always prepared for that reality. For those inclined to care, we stay aware of our own bodies as means to anchor ourselves for hearing secrets. Caring does

---

13. Emma J. Justes, *Please Don't Tell: What to Do with the Secrets People Share* (Nashville: Abingdon Press, 2014), 4.

not mean we need to take on the burden of the secrets. We do stand in a position to accompany a person or group on the journey to release the hold of secrets and to engage in life-giving future choices in behavior and relationships. Emma Justes puts it this way: "*Our being available to hear sometimes horrible secrets and still treasure the secret keeper is essential to moving the secret telling toward becoming a means of grace.*"[14] In caregiving, we ground ourselves in the recognition of our own and other's core humanity since secrets can lead to disdain and judgment. As people committed to embody covenant loyalty, we listen to the release of secrets as a first step on the path toward right relationship.

Key awareness: Learning to tolerate feeling unsettled or somewhat anxious allows us to stay open to listening. Since our brains are wired for survival, we can misread anxiety and psychological discomfort with physical danger as the brain sends out a signal, depending on the situation, to do one of the following: fight, flee, or freeze. We refrain from shaming and blaming and instead engage the proactive posture of befriending our bodies, which expands capacity for being with discomfort.[15] Think of the practice as body hospitality.

> **Tend and Befriend Your Body Practice**
>
> This is a quiet and unnoticeable exercise that can be engaged in one-on-one conversation or in a group setting. Touch the index finger with the thumb on each hand. Notice your breathing. Now, touch the middle finger with the thumb on each hand. Again, notice your breathing. Most people experience taking deeper breaths with the thumbs and middle fingers touching. When you find yourself in a situation with developing body tension and anxiety, engage this practice. It is one way to tend and befriend your body.

Stories of Buried Secrets

Buried family secrets surface in many ways. We may accidentally stumble into them during a conversation, find evidence in a familiar place, or hear news from a relative. The stories usually catch us by surprise.

---

14. Justes, *Please Don't Tell*, 141, italics in original.

15. Storm Swain shared this insight with me as well as the following practice that she learned from a colleague.

Chapter 8

A neighbor shared an exchange between family members that signaled buried family secrets. Her uncle mistook a statement from a colleague as an unsolicited advance toward a member of his family. "Something inside him seemed to blow up, and he shot back quickly: 'How would you like me to talk about a member of your family like that? How would you like me to have an affair or talk about sex with a member of your family?'" The anger and tension she witnessed was palpable. The colleague seemed genuinely caught off guard by the response but didn't become defensive. He then said to her uncle, "I am sorry. I did not mean to hurt or offend you." "Thank you. We're good," her uncle responded. She suspects her uncle and family are still grappling with the ripple effects of an unresolved family secret just coming to consciousness.

Exposing and listening to shameful secrets involves caring and transformation, but it usually may not seem like it. We may make a remark or stumble into a conversation that instigates a surprising response. I once asked a class what it's like to be present with someone as the tentacles of a secret get hooked. "Like a bomb going off," one person quickly replied. Together we pondered how secrets shift internal tectonic plates in our body story and release tension-filled energy with great force. Bombs go off and earthquakes erupt often without warning. Yet alerts occur and we may notice them if we pay attention. Sometimes, others or we ourselves share pieces of a secret and then step back from further investigation of the complete story and its implications. It is a process like venting or letting off steam, which feels good and provides temporary relief. Any piece of work we do by tapping and transforming shameful secrets lessens personal and social burdens now and in the future. Whether as bearers of secrets or those privileged to hear those of others, we participate in step-by-step change. Emma Justes reminds us that we need people and communities generous enough "to receive secrets and stay in relationship."[16] As listeners, we ground ourselves by cultivating body presence so we are less likely to be thrown off balance and more likely to provide an adaptive and flexible response. Body practices connect us with the Healing Source. The psalmist declares: "There is a river whose streams gladden God's city, the holiest

---

16. Justes, *Please Don't Tell*, 98.

dwelling of the Most High" (46:4). We can tap this underground river that nourishes all of life here and available now within our very bodies.

> **Family Secrets and Stories**
>
> In my introduction to pastoral care class, I require participants to complete a genogram, which is a map of family relationships across several generations, and reflect on how those relationships shape them. It is an exercise meant to cultivate awareness and to inform positive leadership practices and professional development. In every class, a few students find the exercise emotionally challenging because of what they discover about family relationships. Some fret about sharing their family's "dirty laundry." I assure them the exercise is confidential. One student remarked somewhat jokingly, "It's your fault that my family is upset with me. But I have found out some things I didn't know." While the exercise was not easy, the student learned through the process.
>
> **Care Practice to Protect the Vulnerable**
>
> We need to take secrets and negative silence seriously. We need to take immediate action, if we learn the following: abuse and neglect of children and the elderly or a person's intention to take one's own life or to harm or to injure another person. Contact professional services in a local jurisdiction. Even if we are not a "mandated reporter" according to the law, it is still our responsibility as people of faith and informed citizens to protect the vulnerable. Here's a practice for care: when listening to difficult experiences and stories, we can believe people are in pain and act on their behalf.

Community Practice

We expose secrets and surface negative silences as individuals. We also need to do it as embodied community. The Johari window was developed as a tool to help individuals develop awareness about themselves and relationships with others (see chart below).[17] From a list of adjectives on a sheet of paper, each person in a group selects the words they think best describe them. Everyone selects adjectives from the same list to describe each person in the group. Insight comes in the connections

---

17. Joseph Luft and Harry Ingham, "The Johari Window, a Graphic Model of Interpersonal Awareness," in *Proceedings of the Western Training Laboratory in Group Development* (Los Angeles: UCLA, 1955).

and disconnections between how we perceive ourselves and how others perceive us. The exercise might be used more than once in a group's life.

	Known to Others	Not Known to Others
Known to Self	**Open:** Stories shared	**Hidden:** Stories private
Not Known to Self	**"Blocked Spot":** Not self-aware; others share stories	**Unknown:** Stories and experience are unconscious

We want to share stories that are conscious and not-yet-revealed, but could be shared with the support of trusting conditions (top half of the grid: stories that are known to self and not known to others). Skilled and licensed helping professionals should be engaged when navigating terrain not known to self and others (the bottom half of the grid). Be prepared for the possible uncomfortable experience of discovering and sharing sensitive and secret stories. Recognize that shameful secrets and negative silence can surround experience in any of the four quadrants. Develop a secure base by doing the following: cultivating trust; practicing confidentiality while recognizing public spaces are never fully "safe"; allowing experience and stories to surface.

In churches and communities oriented toward exposing social secrets and negative silences, a revision of the Johari Window can be a useful tool for growth in community awareness and transformation toward justice.

	Known to Community	Not Known to Community
Known to Church	**Open:** Stories shared	**Hidden:** Stories private and shared only with members
Not Known to Church	**"Blocked Spot":** Not aware; community tells stories about the church	**Unknown:** Stories and experience are unconscious to members and the community

The churh or group as a whole may select a list of adjectives to describe itself. The church or group can examine how and where its identity is embodied in programs and images. For example, a church that chooses "justice-oriented," "welcoming," and "diverse" would look for evidence of that description in community composition and practices. A leadership team or outside consultant or community group could select from a list of adjectives to describe the church. Fruitful conversation and learning come when comparing the lists and noting overlaps and disconnections. A survey is another means to get feedback and to grow in consciousness. The key is to act based on insight and learning.

> **Reflection for Awareness and Justice**
>
> **For Individuals:** What embodied qualities are important when you seek someone out to share your story? How do you know it's time to reveal a hidden story? Have you encountered being given feedback/information that allows for surfacing an unknown aspect of yourself?
>
> **For Groups:** The Johari Window was developed for self-awareness with individuals. Use it as a tool for developing group awareness. What stories are known inside the community but are not shared outside? What are the reasons for this practice? Identify possible steps to narrow the gap between group practice and community perception.
>
> What policies and practices are in place to ensure the safety of all bodies? What policies and practices are in place to deal with exposure of harmful secrets?

Body Honesty

Denial

Denial is an attempt to stay unconscious, a refusal to let information surface that disturbs or interrupts a familiar life pattern. Those who grew up or live in a household with an alcoholic know the extent to which family members can adjust and accommodate to destructive behavior in order to maintain some semblance of equilibrium.[18] It's not healthy, but change also takes effort. Denial, then, can be understood in a couple of ways: (1) intentionally choosing not to see or choosing to look in another direction; (2) not being ready to see because the capacity is lacking to work with what is discovered. Denial can be an initial defense mechanism to protect from potential harm. However, when it becomes the default mode of response, we end up passively reinforcing the status quo.[19]

> **Surfacing Practice**
>
> Denial buries issues. It's procrastination on steroids. The mind says, "This is too big and overwhelming. I'll deal with it later." Later morphs into never. This tendency exacerbates the power of secrets and oppressive systemic patterns. How, then, to work with it? Connect with a friend or trusted accountability partner. Open your heart, and ask of yourself in God's presence: What am I afraid of facing? See what surfaces. Honor it. Say: I can allow this to be exposed to light. Commit to regular surfacing practice, taking one step at a time.

We cover over, deny, and reinforce secrets and negative silences because we fail to acknowledge the deeper connected reality that calls us together. The Apostle Paul in 1 Corinthians 12 uses the body as metaphor for his own rhetorical purpose in addressing the dynamics of a particular community. Undergirding the metaphor is a playful God that delights in creation and humanity in its splendid diversity and unity. In fact, modern science also provides evidence for the deeper reality of human existence. The genome project has demonstrated that the "base-pair level of your genome is 99.9 percent the same as all of the humans around you."[20] May we learn to value and celebrate our similarities and differences at the genome and cultural levels.

---

18. For a helpful resource on caring for addiction, see Sonia A. Waters, *Addiction and Pastoral Care* (Grand Rapids: Eerdmans, 2019). Waters does not use the language of denial. She outlines "Stages of Change Map" based on Change Theory. "Precontemplation" is the first stage during which "the addict does not believe that she has a problem or is not motivated to change" (p. 153).

19. Robin DiAngelo, *White Fragility* (New York: Beacon, 2018), 46. DiAngelo argues that white people often respond with "anger and denial" in response to being called out for "racially problematic" speech and action. This blocks the path toward personal and social change.

20. See "Human Genomic Variation," accessed May 8, 2021, www.genome.gov/dna-day/15-ways/human-genomic-variation.

Defenses

Those in dominant cultural groups need to notice and to stay with our defenses. Being defensive or emotionally reactive says: "I am not willing to sit with the pain in my body listening to this story or experience prompts." We may encounter our own shame or sense of deficiency, powerlessness, need to please, or failure to exercise control, among others.[21] The inability to see our own experience of shame confines us to blaming ourselves or others and locks us in defensive mode. We lose an opportunity to get to the root of what is bothersome. A pause or interruption allows for "being with" the uncomfortable or unsettling matter. We rest into the secure base of our bodies and trust we are creatures blessed as God's beloved, able to learn from mistakes, and capable of taking positive action for others and ourselves.[22]

> **Practices: Interrupt and Interrogate Body Reactivity**
>
> **Personal Reflection:** Ponder an experience when you found yourself defensive. Did it occur as you were listening or reading or otherwise not actively engaged with others, or did it occur in direct interaction with one or more others? What was it like internally for you? What beliefs about yourself were challenged?
>
> **Interpersonal Practice:** Defensiveness often occurs when receiving criticism and feedback from others. Reactivity can also be magnified depending on how communication occurs. Taking proactive steps lessens interpersonal tensions and contributes to open communication, mutual learning, and team-building. "Fogging," or non-defensive listening and responding practice, is outlined below.[23]
>
> When receiving criticism, name the truth in another person's critical statements: (1) you can agree with any statement that is true for you; (2) you can agree with any statement that may contain some truth; or (3) you can agree with any statement that is a generalization, as long as it has some possibility of being true for you.

---

21. Edward Wimberly uses the term *myths* to describe how beliefs about self are developed and shape behavior. See Edward P. Wimberly, *Recalling Our Own Stories: Spiritual Renewal for Religious Caregivers* (Minneapolis: Fortress, 2019).

22. The term *secure base* comes from the work of British psychiatrist John Bowlby and refers to nurturing, supportive, and welcoming provisions for development that parents and caregivers establish in the home so that children and adolescents grow in the capacity to venture into the world with confidence. See John Bowlby, *A Secure Base: Parent-Child Attachment and Healthy Human Development* (New York: Basic Books, 1988), 11.

23. John Savage, *Listening and Caring Skills: A Guide for Groups and Leaders* (Nashville: Abingdon Press, 1996), 57–62.

Non-defensive practice figures prominently in my teaching as a white male instructor who desires to model respect and vulnerability in the multicultural classroom with its student diversity in terms of class, gender, race, sexual orientation, and ability. As we are able, we all need to work against patterns that fuel secrecy and negative stereotypes. In the class, an open invitation to contemplative body practice allows students to decide for themselves if and how they want to participate. An African American student once said he did not close his eyes while doing the practice because where he grew up it could be dangerous to do so. He voiced the need to protect his Black body, a response based in fear that others in the room also experienced. This body reality challenges an assumption that spiritual practice takes only one form (e.g., eyes closed and heads bowed). My own identity as a white-embodied instructor was shaped by this encounter: I noticed what was happening in my body during the conversation and did not become defensive, and simultaneously opened space for students of color, in particular, and others to claim their bodily experience. In teaching and ministries of care, we need to maximize such moments in order to cultivate open communication and honor diverse body identities.

Paul's Body Metaphor

Paul's body metaphor in 1 Corinthians 12 upends the assumed social hierarchy and casts a vision for just and harmonious relationship; see verses 23-24: "The parts of the body that we think are less honorable are the ones we honor the most. The private parts of our bodies that aren't presentable are the ones that are given the most dignity. The parts of our bodies that are presentable don't need this. But God has put the body together, giving greater honor to the part with less honor." Social divisions existed in the church at Corinth just as they exist to varying degrees in churches and communities today. But the church as the body of Christ calls for a different kind of ordering. We might call Paul a playful prophet.[24] He criticizes the status quo of unequal divisions even as he creatively imagines a new possibility of harmonious relationships. The church body—the community as a whole—functions as the body of Christ as it reorders social divisions and values all, not just some, members of the community. No doubt those in positions of power and privilege do not take kindly to this word. The ego functions of power, privilege, and status mostly want to squelch the message. The image calls people from conflict to transformative care: "So that there won't be division in the body and so the parts might have mutual concern for each other. If one part suffers, all the parts suffer with it; if one part gets the glory, all the parts celebrate with it" (vv. 25-26).

Paul's body metaphor emphasizes the care practice of mutual concern. No *one* should be marginalized for *who they are* as part of the body. Minimizing the part also diminishes the whole. The metaphor also unifies as it recognizes difference: "We were all baptized by one Spirit into one body, whether Jew or Greek, or slave or free, and we all were given one Spirit to drink" (1 Cor 12:13). Paul casts a vision for the church and spiritual communities to become egalitarian and nonhierarchical contexts for social relationships.[25] The theological vision also beckons for expansion in multifaith contexts. All people who seek the common good contribute to the embodiment of love, one of the greatest things according to Paul (cf. 1 Cor 13:13). What does the metaphor suggest for care? **Reflect:** Imagine what valuing each member of the body entails in your context. How does "mutual concern" reframe the inclination toward giving and getting special treatment only for a select group? How might the spiritual community as the body of Christ serve and value "all parts of the body," those inside as well as those outside its border?

Process theologians envision God as One who calls humanity to creative adventure. God interrelates with all occasions of experience, knows all possibilities, and lures us to make choices that embody flourishing for

---

24. Paul invites "playfulness and humor" to drive his theological points in this chapter. See Charles Campbell, *1 Corinthians* (Louisville: Westminster John Knox, 2018), 205–11.

25. Victor Turner refers to egalitarian and nonhierarchical social relationships as *communitas*. See *The Ritual Process: Structure and Anti-Structure* (New York: Aldine de Gruyter, 1995), 96–97.

ourselves and the world. God is on the side of actual creativity, novelty, diversity, and harmony, not as abstractions but as embodied realities. This theology also recognizes that each moment arises along with the massive weight of the past. Creative choice is possible but is not always probable. We need to reckon with history that includes deeply ingrained patterns of behavior in ourselves and others. So, what separates us from the love of God is not who we are but what we choose to do or not to do.

Instinctive Wisdom

On a hot summer day, I observed a dog and its owner on a walk when the dog "decided" to plop on the road under a shade tree, a physical refusal to continue walking. The owner was not sympathetic. She tried to pick the dog up and place its paws down as if she were teaching a toddler to walk. It was quite a scene. This big gentle dog did not budge. The dog was in touch with its body. Instinctive wisdom says, "No walking. It's too hot and hurts the paws." Instinctual wisdom is the story our bodies tell, too, if we listen. Like the dog lying in the shade on a hot day, our bodies give clues for the right thing to do.

Being out of touch with instinctual wisdom comes at a cost to our personal and social well-being. We stop seeing who we are and who others are as beloved of God. We objectify and separate. We create categories of superiority and inferiority. "A house divided against itself, cannot stand," Abraham Lincoln warned in a speech regarding slavery delivered in his campaign for the presidency.[26] The words echo Jesus's warning in Matthew 12:25: "Every kingdom involved in civil war becomes a wasteland. Every city or house torn apart by divisions will collapse." As people of conscience and faith, we need draw on the Spirit of God to halt and to heal divisions. We see the devastating effects of divided thinking played out in history and within our cultures, workplaces, and churches.

---

26. Abraham Lincoln, "House Divided" speech, June 16, 1858.

> **Practicing with Instinctive Body Wisdom**
>
> Listening to stories of pain and trauma requires staying grounded in body wisdom. A hospital chaplain tells of caring for a patient grieving the deaths of close family members and struggling to stay on the path to recovery. The patient poured out her story and then asked: "What should I do?" It seemed to be a statement of desperation rather than an invitation to respond. While refraining from giving advice, the chaplain instead noticed how the interaction hooked his feelings of anxiety and sadness, valuable clues into the patient's experience. The chaplain created space for the patient to express herself. Rather than being concerned with saying the right thing, the chaplain instead tuned in to his own body's instinctual wisdom to chart the path through caring presence. "I paid attention to my feet while listening. It made me feel centered and anchored."
>
> Practice instinctual body wisdom for yourself. Pay attention to your feet. Notice how reaching out a hand may help. Sit rather than standing, or stand rather than sitting. Take a deep, intentional breath to release built-up tension. Identify a time when practicing instinctual wisdom has helped you or another person.

Body Care Prayer

God of Silence and Speech,
You love humanity and creation as a whole and in all its parts. Through nurturing silence and in bold action and speech, you beckon us to take up the work of advocacy and justice: to expose and transform negative secrets so that your new story of diversity and inclusion may be realized. You see creation and humanity as puzzle pieces that fit together with exquisite beauty. Where we can only see disparate parts, you call us to imagine the whole. When we opt to distance ourselves and shade over differences, you also call us to focus fine attention on the parts. Energize us, O Spirit of Life, to hold the whole and to tend to the pieces as we become embodied advocates of loving and humanizing justice practices for all.
Amen.

Chapter 9

CONCLUSION: BEING HOME

Late one August night in 1987, I arrived exhausted at my parents' home. I had just returned from China the previous week where I had spent the year teaching English. The following week I planned to begin my theological studies at Yale Divinity School. But the evening was spent with friends and ministers beginning to process our grief after a friend's death by suicide. Earlier that day, a close friend from college was discovered hanging in his bedroom.

My mother met me at the front door and gave me a big hug. "Welcome home," she said. I walked to the back patio where my father was pacing, trying to make sense of the tragedy. "Why did he do it?" my father asked. I had no words. The question has lingered for years as I, too, have wrestled with it. I know this: mental anguish and torment overwhelmed Bill's ability to function. His body had become a prison of suffering. He wanted to escape.

Not everyone receives a welcome home or experiences their body as home. That stark reality has stayed with me since Bill's death. Some of us struggle with mental health issues. Others live in social circumstances that render their bodies invisible, foreign, problematic. Care of our bodies is essential spiritual work that we do for the benefit of others and for ourselves. It allows us to respond to the One who builds a house and invites us into abundant life.

Chapter 9

Contexts of Home

"Welcome home" is a message we can practice saying to ourselves and with seekers in care. The deep irony is that Bill did not feel welcome in his own body. Suicide is a way out of a body that feels nothing like home. Others, too, know this alienating reality. Thomas Burke, a veteran who served tours of duty in Iraq and Afghanistan, gives voice to the mental and physical anguish that engulfed him. He "describes his near suicide as a physical reaction to unrelenting stress. 'My body wanted to kill itself—which is very alien, for an animal to want to self-destruct.'" A comrade fortunately stopped him before he could carry through with shooting himself.[1] Burke suffered with PTSD (post-traumatic stress disorder) and experienced what theological scholars have identified as "moral injury." Moral injury names the suffering of mind and body that occurs when people observe or participate in acts that violate core beliefs.[2]

As ministers and care seekers, we ought not romanticize the notion of "being at home" in the body. Social stigmas and internalized negative messages prohibit the ability for some to be comfortably home. Pushed to the side and made to feel less than human, marginalized and oppressed people know this reality all too well. This is not just a personal problem but also is reflective of social disease. We all need to wrestle and reckon with messages that render some bodies subordinate and others dominant and privileged. Some of those messages have been taught in our churches and spiritual communities. We need to rewrite them in light of God's care for all persons and with a preferential option for those who are marginalized and outcast.

Pastoral leaders, spiritual directors, and counselors are frontline workers. We witness directly how people bump up against practices that attempt to deny, erase, and overlook their bodily existence. This occurs, in part, because texts and traditions are embedded in biased and limited

---

1. Cathy Shufro, "War and After: Veterans of Recent Conflicts Talk about Their Lives Before and After Deployment," *Yale Alumni Magazine*, May/June 2016, 52.

2. For helpful resources on moral injury, see the following: Rita Nakashima Brock and Gabriella Lettini, *Soul Repair: Recovering from Moral Injury after War* (Boston: Beacon, 2013); Larry Kent Graham, *Moral Injury: Restoring Wounded Souls* (Nashville: Abingdon Press, 2017).

worldviews. While the Hebrew Bible or Old Testament "maintains a more wholesome view of the entire body 'complex' (i.e., it does not divide persons into 'soul' and 'body,' but sees them as a unity), [it] is deeply fearful of women's bodies and the power of procreation and blood which they hold."[3] The New Testament presents deeper challenges as the "apocalyptic worldview and affirmation of a Savior embodied in *male* (*not* female) form caused its writers to place a low valuation on female embodiment, and its anthropology does see a 'soul/body' split."[4] Ancient texts and religious traditions have contexts and histories we need to analyze thoroughly before we adopt wholesale the messages they convey about bodies. My hope is that we claim our own bodily integrity and worth and interpret scripture and church/religious traditions in light of a worldview in which God affirms the blessings of all bodies and not just some. Challenge any story or practice that denigrates the body and reimagine new life-giving possibilities.

A client shared a dream image about a slanted house. Here is the gist of it. While walking around a beautiful garden, she is invited inside a house and notices how strange it seems: the furnishings and cabinetry all slope downward. "Everything is slightly off," Sheila blurted out. The therapist imagined an amusement park "fun house" that plays with the mind through distortion and disorientation. "I usually enjoy these mind tricks," Sheila grinned, "but I didn't like this one." I wondered how it left her feeling when she awoke. "Sad," she admitted. "The garden is so beautiful and the house looks great on the outside. But, the inside, well . . . it needs work." I wondered if she saw the need to put the house in order. "Yes, that's it!" she exclaimed.

Sheila sees the need to get her house in order. For her, the inside needs work. We may find ourselves at a similar threshold. Here's the good news: getting our houses in order does not mean getting them perfect, but rather putting in the effort to care. The slanted-house image calls to mind the way that leads to destruction, personified as Woman Stranger, in Proverbs chapters 1–8. The biblical wisdom tradition is about the search for God-

---

3. Carole R. Fontaine, *With Eyes of Flesh: The Bible, Gender and Human Rights* (Sheffield, UK: Sheffield Phoenix, 2008), 154.

4. Fontaine, *With Eyes of Flesh*, 154.

given order in the world. Basically, the acts/consequence theology offers two ways. Woman Wisdom personifies the path of the righteous while Woman Stranger shows the way to destruction. The feminine figures serve as an appeal to the book's male-dominated audience. Wisdom delights before God and takes joy in the world; Woman Wisdom herself "is at 'the center of a matrix of relationships'—a vital bridge between God, humans, and the world."[5] Our bodies are a "house" in which we make a home with God as we live out covenant commitments and share blessings with others. Woman Wisdom welcomes all.

The death-dealing way presents as alluring and seductive, yet it does not offer satisfaction. We cannot live abundantly in a house that is uninhabitable. Body practices, too, can be pursued for either shallow or purposeful ends. The outside can be seen as just "for appearances" and also represents the interface between living our deepest values and having them seen by others. The inside can be seen as our private space; it is also where we may need assistance if we struggle with mental illness or wrestle with questions of identity and self-worth. God's "welcome home" beckons us all. How will we respond?

Healing Ecosystems

A popular bumper sticker reads: "Think Globally, Act Locally." It calls us to make connections between the care, health, and well-being of our bodies and larger systems. Imbalances in ecosystems create problems for the planet and for all inhabitants. This is a body problem. Howard Clinebell argues that we need to move from "ecoalienation" to "ecobonding" in individual and collective practices. "Ecoalienation involves seeking to distance oneself from our inescapable life-giving dependence on nature." All the ways we ignore, deny, or reject our connection with the earth reflects our ecoalienation. Ecobonding, the healing alternative vision, "involves claiming and enjoying one's nurturing, energizing, life-enhancing connectedness with nature."[6]

---

5. Christine Roy Yoder, "Proverbs," in *Women's Bible Commentary*, ed. Newsom, Ringe, and Lapsley, 236.

6. Howard Clinebell, *Ecotherapy: Healing Ourselves, Healing the Earth* (Minneapolis: Augsburg Fortress, 1996), 26.

Conclusion: Being Home

A boat ride on the Anacostia River offers an opportunity to learn directly about ecoalienation and a nonprofit organization's mission to promote ecobonding with local communities.[7] The river is part of a watershed, an area of land that drains creeks and streams that stretch across three jurisdictions in the Washington, DC area. Through many years of neglect, the river has become devastated with pollution and waste. Effort is underway to halt and reverse that tragic course. Strategies include restoring the river as a source of recreation, advocating for policies that protect and invigorate the health of the watershed, teaching local communities about the river's importance in the larger ecosystem and its interdependence with their health and well-being, and stewarding planting and rain water projects to revitalize the river.

When we care for our bodies, we grow in our desire to learn about and promote the health of larger ecosystems. The watershed's health intersects with the health and vitality of surrounding communities. As care seekers, we can engage "ecotherapy" practices at work, at home, in our church communities, and in our neighborhoods. All efforts, at every level, make a difference: removing Styrofoam and plastic from use; advocating for a tax on bags and banning plastic; planting a rain garden; and learning from books and experts about the interconnections between environmental justice, racial and economic disparities, and body health.

We can interpret revitalization of the watershed in terms of Christian theology: the river symbolizes both the death and devastation of the cross and the real transformed possibilities of resurrection. The river also flows as part of an interdependent web of creation. Spiritual seekers and communities can adopt their own mission statement with regard to ecotherapy and justice to mend the web in their location. Everyone can start where they are. My mother and her next-door neighbor take daily walks through their neighborhood. They carry bags to collect bottles and cans along the way. It is a simple ecological body practice that energizes them. It also cleans up the environment and leaves an impression on others. This is one small example of acting locally.

---

7. The educational and recreational outreach occurred through the Anacostia Watershed Society (www.anacostiaws.org).

Chapter 9

> **Micro Body Practices**
>
> No practice is insignificant if it connects us with God, self, and others. "Micro-practices" include observing, appreciating, and doing anything good for the body in a few minutes or less. Waiting for coffee to brew allows for a few repetitions of lifting ten-pound weights. Stopping at a red light offers an opportunity for intentional deep breathing. Standing in line at the grocery creates a moment to give thanks for food that nourishes our bodies. Drawing a finger labyrinth focuses attention during online meetings. Rolling a ball under the feet relieves stress.
>
> Each day brings new learning for body and mind. Observe, appreciate, and do what you can for yourself and your ecosystem. Develop your own practices and share ideas with others.

Breathe, Just Breathe

Breath work can help bring us together in a fragmented world. Breath awareness is often associated with Eastern meditation practices and can be dismissed by some people as "out there" or "New Age." I learned this long ago while writing a column for a college newspaper. One piece generated a lot of response. I suggested that Jesus would have conversation with those practicing the spirituality of the New Age movement. This comment was meant to underscore a point: traditional religion sometimes excludes people and leaves spiritual yearning unaddressed. This is unfortunate.

If we define ourselves as "not that," then we lose the opportunity to learn or to reclaim practices that serve well-being. Breath is essential for life and the base of many practices introduced throughout this book. We connect with our breath as an embodied practice to support life. We hear the cry "I can't breathe" as a spiritual wake-up call for social reform to ensure justice, especially for Black, Brown, and Asian bodies.

Our breath indicates how we really are. In care with others, we do not always have to ask people how they are feeling. We can observe their breathing and get a sense of things. Breathing rhythm provides a clue to emotional states such as agitation, anxiety, calm, fear, and worry. This is a clue the rest of the body corroborates. In care situations, we can pay attention to our own breathing in order to stay in touch with our bodies and sense the emotional states of other bodies. Breath awareness and practice anchors us within our bodies and grounds us for caring relationships with others.

Noticing and Deepening the Breath

Put attention on the breath and simply observe. This is itself a powerful action. The key is not to exert too much force. Noticing and observing can on their own unfold into allowing the breath gradually to lengthen. Begin meetings, prayer, preaching, and teaching with this practice. This can be a step by itself and can also be used as a segue to full breathing. Relaxed and full breathing allows for equal and complete inhalation and exhalation. If we are still, "a full breath must be taken slowly, no more than eight a minute, to avoid hyperventilation."[8] We can model and practice with others.

In care conversations, allow yourself to engage in breathing that expands and contracts with ease. It is not necessary to foster deep breathing since that can take attention away from the care seeker and is more conducive to prayerful meditation. Make an effort to be fully present and responsive in conversation. Check in with breathing at the beginning and then intermittently throughout an interaction. I recommend this practice to stay with our own bodies as a guide in care. That way, we do not slip into offering "head" responses that tend toward the "fix it" mode of care. We awaken our bodies and intuitive awareness to the fullest possible sense of another person's experience.

Spiritual care interactions can transpire quickly, so we need to be prepared. A congregant walked up to me during coffee hour and expressed a bit of a recent interaction with her son-in-law. I got the sense she was trying to be helpful and received rebuke. "You're feeling hurt by that comment," I said in response to Dinah's story. She did not say, "I was hurt,"

---

8. Brian Bair, "Breathing for a Better World," in *The Revelation of the Breath: A Tribute to Its Wisdom, Power, and Beauty* (Albany, NY: SUNY, 2009), 245.

but breath awareness helped me hear and feel what she was saying. "Yes, I was," Dinah said quietly before pausing and moving on with her story. Intentional breathing makes us more likely to catch feelings and thoughts that might otherwise float by.

Breath Problems

Shallow breathing and holding the breath are two common problems most of us encounter in our breathing rhythm. "A shallow breath is a small, unconscious breath taken ten or more times a minute into the upper part of the lungs with a very slight physical movement."[9] When we use only a small fraction of our lung capacity, may experience muscle tension and feel fatigued. Holding the breath occurs when the exhalation is halted. "After breathing out, but not completely, the breath stops for several seconds." Holding the breath is a physical response to an emotional experience.[10] We are, in effect, refusing to be where we are or to be doing what we are doing. I sometimes hold my breath before meetings. It is a body message that says, "I don't want to go or deal with the emotions that get stirred up."

Neither shallow breathing nor holding the breath serves our connection with God, ourselves, and one another. Notice and return to relaxed, intentional breathing. Use soothing self-talk to ease resistance with phrases such as "it's okay," "I don't need to fight this," and "I don't need to brace myself." Pay attention, though, to the patterns of resistance and refusals because they signal something about how we are investing our life energy. Perhaps changes are in order.

Humming, singing, or listening to music can all be helpful accompaniments to breath work. The hymn "Breathe on Me, Breath of God" is one I use to release inner defenses and ease into God's presence.[11] Discover what works for you.

---

9. Bair, "Breathing for a Better World," 245.
10. Bair, "Breathing for a Better World," 245.
11. See *The United Methodist Hymnal* (Nashville: Abingdon Press, 1989), 420.

Conclusion: Being Home

Steady and Flexible Rule

In the fifth century, Saint Benedict established a "rule" with detailed guidance for living, praying, and working together in monastic community. Christian communities over centuries and across cultures have modified the rule that orders life. For a monastic community, the rule includes systems of accountability and structures to ensure that individual members and the community as a whole fulfills vows of stability, fidelity to the monastic way of life, and obedience.[12]

As spiritual seekers and caregivers, we benefit from "a rule" to order our lives as well. The rule might be a system of accountability that includes spiritual coaches, colleagues, and companions to support the commitment to engage body practices. I responded affirmatively to constitutional questions when I was ordained to the ministry thirty years ago. I also felt a sense of yearning for a deeper spiritual life and made a vow to daily practice and reflection. In recent years, I have added the vow to care for my own body and others' bodies as part of God's call to wholeness.

The seeds for current practice were planted in the early 1990s. I attended a ten-day retreat with Christians and other spiritual seekers with practices of silent meditation, yoga, and community building. The body practices have continued as my primary practices for almost three decades. Every morning I follow this practice: ten minutes of yoga postures, ten minutes of scripture reading from the daily lectionary, and twenty-five minutes of quiet prayer. It is the first thing I do in the morning, always before eating breakfast, reading the paper, and checking the internet and email. I have varied the routine but have always included quiet body prayer. I used to do yoga at other times during the day but realized I needed to engage the postures first. Easing stiffness and releasing tension in the body through yoga postures settles and opens my body, mind, and spirit to God's presence and insights from scripture.

Choose practices that "fit." We need to try practices on like we would try on a piece of clothing, and ask ourselves: Does this fit? How does it

---

12. For a thoughtful interpretive guide to the rule, see Joan Chittister, *A Spirituality for the 21st Century: The Rule of Benedict* (New York: Crossroad, 2010).

work for me? Other people cannot truly tell what works for us. Still, they can provide helpful feedback that we're on the right path. The spouse of a student commented, "Whatever you've been doing, keep at it!" That is surely an indication the practice fits.

In challenging times and crisis moments, we need trustworthy practice to see us through. The Chinese character for crisis is composed of the pictographs for "danger" and "opportunity" together. Through body practices, we navigate both aspects of the Mandarin word. For spiritual seekers, a couple of dangers include latching on to simplistic explanations of reality or feeling futile about it all. We can instead choose to delve deeper and rely on life-giving body practices to show us the way.

Platitudes are simple statements that stifle further exploration as they reduce complexity to simplicity. Examples include phrases such as, "It could be worse," "She is in a better place," and "Look on the bright side." We can use the Bible and other sacred literature in a proof-texting manner by selecting a quotation and applying it to a situation without consideration of the passage's or the listener's context. People are not comforted, and much harm can occur through the use of these seemingly innocuous remarks. In a time of crisis, we realize how unsatisfying a platitude can be. Platitudes run roughshod over experience. They put a happy face on matters. Yet another possibility exists. The poet Rumi muses: "Out beyond ideas of wrongdoing and rightdoing, there is a field. I'll meet you there."[13] Spiritual practice allows for holding the both/and together instead of denying the negative or forcing the positive. It is the field of being and heart of pastoral and spiritual caring.

During the early months of the global pandemic, a podcast interviewer asked advice on "rethinking" leadership care practices. We should not "over-think" what we do, and thereby miss making connections to difficult emotions. A pastor and former student communicated how much he appreciated the assertion. We need practices that can hold us together since many people are, in his words, "operating in a type of panic mode that is causing an overload to our systems." In crisis, there are many pos-

---

13. Jalal al-Din Rumi, *The Essential Rumi*, expanded ed., trans. Coleman Barks (San Francisco: HarperOne, 2004), 35.

sible dangers, one of which is to glide over emotions and move straight to our heads. Platitudes, such as, "This, too, shall pass" and "God is bigger than this virus," serve as knee-jerk thought responses that prematurely call the question rather than open conversation. We need to be more intentional in being with our own bodies. That wisdom informs whatever rethinking needs to be done.

Joko Beck, founder and teacher at the Zen Center of San Diego had a no-nonsense, platitude-free style. Her teaching informed practice developed while a PhD student in Claremont, California, and carries forth in teaching pastoral care classes: meditation practice helps to release the thoughts that loop in the mind. Meditation and prayer as opening to God is a kind of unloading of the system. Contemplative prayer and other spiritual practices serve a similar purpose: to let go of the thoughts and tap into God's presence.

Psalm 46 calls for calm amidst creation in chaos and a world in turmoil. "Be still, and know that I am God! I am exalted among the nations, I am exalted in the earth" (v. 10 NRSV). Be still means "to stop, desist, don't do anything." The "being still" at the heart of body practice is not passive acceptance of the status quo. It is a letting go of all that interferes with the genuine presence of God who calls us to embody life-giving possibilities for our communities and for ourselves. "Just be here" is encouragement to practice being with anxiety and realizing its connections. That helps with being less anxious. The world teaches us to keep pushing the "thinking" panic button, but pastoral leaders and care seekers need to model a healing alternative for showing up in the world. We embrace our whole experience regardless of whether we are seething in anger at injustice, fearing for others' and our own lives, grieving losses, or reeling with anxiety. Embodied spiritual practice makes space for it all.

We have all been catapulted into an unfamiliar reality. The abrupt shift to online worship and education presents new dangers and opportunities for body practices. Spiritual seekers, leaders, and teachers need to stay open and watchful as we engage in ministering and learning alongside others. I know that being with fear and anxiety is immensely difficult as agitation stirs in the body. I know being present in and experiencing takes effort. Yet, I also know from years of practice that being still puts us in touch with the energy forces at work within and around us. All is quiet in the eye of the hurricane, but getting there/being here is a challenge.

I began writing this book with a strong sense, touched in my spiritual practice, that my body is not an appendage to spiritual practice. Our bodies are partners in the path. It is a simple thing to state. It is an entirely revolutionary matter to live out since messages in the tradition and in our cultures separate us from our bodies. I conclude this writing amidst a global health pandemic and protests in the United States in response to police killing and violence against Black bodies. The Black Lives Matter movement is this generation's movement to seek racial justice and inclusion for all. Kelly Brown Douglas asserts that the "stand your ground" cultural awakening is a *kairos* moment for the Black community.[14] *Kairos* is the biblical Greek word for "ripe time." Now is the time for all spiritual seekers and communities of care to do our part to embody justice and peace.

---

14. Kelly Brown Douglas, *Stand Your Ground: Black Bodies and the Justice of God* (Maryknoll, NY: Orbis, 2015), 20–22.

Conclusion: Being Home

> **Practice:** Create space and encourage people to try practices on their own. Use reflection time in person and online to process the experiences.
>
> Here is a suggested spiritual practice drawn from various traditions:
>
> Sit in a comfortable position
>
> Notice and let go of all platitudes/thoughts/feelings
>
> Focus on your breath
>
> Acknowledge what's happening in your body

Be still for a while
I'll meet you there in stillness.

Bibliography

Anderson, Herbert and Kenneth R. Mitchell. *Leaving Home.* Louisville: Westminster John Knox, 1993.

Bair, Brian. "Breathing for a Better World." In *The Revelation of the Breath: A Tribute to Its Wisdom, Power, and Beauty*, ed. Sharon G. Mijares, pp. 239–51. Albany: SUNY Press 2009.

Baldwin, Jennifer. *Trauma-Sensitive Theology: Thinking Theologically in the Era of Trauma.* Eugene: Cascade, 2018.

Bass, Diana Butler. *Grounded: Finding God in the World—A Spiritual Revolution.* San Francisco: HarperOne, 2015

Bayda, Ezra. *Being Zen: Bringing Meditations to Life.* Boston: Shambhala, 2002.

Benson, Herbert, and William Proctor. *Relaxation Revolution: Enhancing Your Personal Health Through the Science and Genetics of Mind Body Healing.* New York: Scribner, 2010.

Bidwell, Duane R. *Short-Term Spiritual Guidance.* Minneapolis: Augsburg Fortress Publishers, 2004.

Bob-Waksberg, Raphael. *Some Who Will Love You in All Your Damaged Glory.* New York: Alfred A. Knopf, 2019.

Bourgeault, Cynthia. *Centering Prayer and Inner Awakening.* Boston: Cowley, 2014.

_____. *The Heart of Centering Prayer: Nondual Christianity in Theory and Practice.* Boston: Shambhala, 2016.

Bowlby, John. *A Secure Base: Parent-Child Attachment and Healthy Human Development.* New York: Basic Books, 1988.

Brock, Rita Nakashima and Gabriella Lettini. *Soul Repair: Recovering from Moral Injury after War*. Boston: Beacon, 2013.

Brueggemann, Walter. *Living toward a Vision*. Philadelphia: United Church Press, 1976.

_____. *Reverberations of Faith: A Theological Handbook of Old Testament Themes*. Louisville: Westminster John Knox, 2002.

Buber, Martin. *I and Thou*. trans. Walter Kaufman. New York: Touchstone, 1996.

Bulkeley, Kelly. *Big Dreams: The Science of Dreaming and the Origins of Religion*. New York: Oxford University Press, 2016.

Campbell, Charles. *1 Corinthians*. Louisville: Westminster John Knox, 2018.

Capps, Donald A. *Living Stories: Pastoral Counseling in Congregational Context*. Minneapolis: Fortress, 1998.

Chittister, Joan. *A Spirituality for the 21st Century: The Rule of Benedict*. New York: Crossroad, 2010.

Chodron, Pema. *The Places That Scare You: A Guide to Fearlessness in Difficult Times*. Boston: Shambhala, 2005.

Clinebell, Howard. *Ecotherapy: Healing Ourselves, Healing the Earth*. Minneapolis: Augsburg Fortress, 1996.

Cooper, Karla J. and Joretta L. Marshall. "Where Race, Gender, and Orientation Meet." In *Women Out of Order: Risking Change and Creating Care in a Multicultural World*, ed. Jeanne Stevenson-Moessner and Teresa Snorton, pp. 115–27. Minneapolis: Fortress, 2009.

Cooper-White, Pamela. *Shared Wisdom: Use of the Self in Pastoral Care and Counseling*. Minneapolis: Fortress, 2004.

Cornell, Ann Weiser. *The Power of Focusing: A Practical Guide to Emotional Self-Healing*. Oakland: New Harbinger, 1996.

_____. *Focusing in Clinical Practice: The Essence of Change*. New York: W. W. Norton, 2013.

Csikszentmihalyi, Mihaly. *Creativity: Flow and the Psychology of Discovery and Invention*. New York: HarperCollins, 1996.

DiAgenlo, Robin. *White Fragility: Why It's So Hard for White People to Talk about Racism*. New York: Beacon, 2018.

Douglas, Kelly Brown. *Stand Your Ground: Black Bodies and the Justice of God.* Maryknoll, NY: Orbis, 2015.

Drescher, Elizabeth. *Choosing Our Religion: The Spiritual Lives of America's Nones.* New York: Oxford University Press, 2016.

Fiorenza, Elisabeth Schussler. *Ephesians.* Wisdom Commentary, vol. 50, ed. Linda M. Maloney and Barbara E. Reid. Collegeville, MN: Liturgical, 2017.

Fontaine, Carole R. *With Eyes of Flesh: The Bible, Gender and Human Rights.* Sheffield, UK: Sheffield Phoenix, 2008.

Frank, Arthur W. *The Wounded Storyteller: Body, Illness, and Ethics.* Chicago: University of Chicago Press, 2013.

Freire, Paulo. *Pedagogy of the Oppressed*, 4th ed. London: Bloomsbury Academic, 2018.

Friedman, Lenore and Susan Moon, ed. *Being Bodies: Buddhist Women on the Paradox of Embodiment.* Boston: Shambhala, 1997.

Gawande, Atul. *Being Mortal: Medicine and What Matters in the End.* New York: Henry Holt & Company, 2014.

Geertz, Clifford. *The Interpretation of Cultures.* New York: Basic Books, 1973.

Gendlin, Eugene T. *Focusing.* New York: Bantam, 1981.

Graham, Larry Kent. *Moral Injury: Restoring Wounded Souls.* Nashville: Abingdon Press, 2017.

_____. *Care of Persons, Care of Worlds: A Psychosystems Approach to Pastoral Care and Counseling.* Nashville: Abingdon Press, 1992.

Guenther, Margaret. *Holy Listening: The Art of Spiritual Direction.* Boston: Cowley, 1992.

Habito, Ruben L. F. *Living Zen, Loving God.* Somerville, MA: Wisdom Publications, 1995.

Hall, Charles E. *Head and Heart: The Story of the Clinical Pastoral Education Movement.* Atlanta: Journal of Pastoral Care Publications, 1992.

Hamman, Jaco J. *Growing Down: Theology and Human Nature in the Virtual Age.* Waco, TX: Baylor University Press, 2017.

Hanson, Karen R. "The Midwife." In *Images of Pastoral Care: Classic Readings*, ed. Robert C. Dyktra. St. Louis: Chalice, 2005.

Herman, Judith. *Trauma and Recovery: The Aftermath of Violence—From Domestic Abuse to Political Terror*. New York: Basic Books, 2015.

Heschel, Abraham Joshua. *The Prophets*. New York: Harper & Row, 1962.

Holmes, Barbara A. *Joy Unspeakable: Contemplative Practices of the Black Church*, 2nd ed. Minneapolis: Fortress, 2017.

Hopkins, Denise Dombkowski. *Journey through the Psalms*, rev. and exp. ed. St. Louis: Chalice, 2002.

_____. "Biblical Anthropology, Discipline of." In *Dictionary of Pastoral Care and Counseling*, ed. Hunter, Rodney J. Hunter, pp. 85–88. Nashville: Abingdon Press, 2005.

Hopkins, Denise Dombkowski and Michael S. Koppel. *Grounded in the Living Word: The Old Testament and Pastoral Care Practices*. Grand Rapids: Wm. B. Eerdmans, 2010.

Hunsinger, Deborah van Deusen and Theresa F. Latini. *Transforming Church Conflict: Compassionate Leadership in Action*. Louisville: Westminster John Knox, 2013.

Hunsinger, Deborah van Deusen. *Bearing the Unbearable: Trauma, Gospel, and Pastoral Care*. Grand Rapids: Wm. B. Eerdmans, 2015.

Justes, Emma J. *Hearing beyond the Words: How to Become a Listening Pastor*. Nashville: Abingdon Press, 2006.

_____. *Please Don't Tell: What to Do with the Secrets People Share*. Nashville: Abingdon Press, 2014.

Kaufman, Sarah L. *The Art of Grace: On Moving through Life*. New York: W. W. Norton, 2016.

Keating, Thomas. *Foundations for Centering Prayer and the Christian Contemplative Life: Open Mind, Open Heart; Invitation to Love; The Mystery of Christ*. New York: Continuum, 2002.

_____. *Intimacy with God: An Introduction to Centering Prayer*. New York: Crossroad, 2009.

Kelly, Melissa M. *Grief: Contemporary Theory in the Practice of Ministry* Minneapolis: Fortress, 2010.

Kendi, Ibrahim X. *How to Become an Antiracist*. London: Oneworld, 2019.

Kleinman, Arthur and Joan Kleinman. "How Bodies Remember: Social Memory and Bodily Experience of Criticism, Resistance, and Delegitimation Following China's Cultural Revolution." *New Literary History* 25 (1994): 710–11.

Koppel, Michael S. "Companions in Presence: Animal Assistants and Eldercare." *Pastoral Psychology* 60, no. 1 (2011): 107–15.

———. "The Prophets and Pastoral Care." In *The Oxford Handbook of the Prophets*, ed. Carolyn J. Sharp. Oxford: Oxford University Press, 2016.

Kornfeld, Margaret. *Cultivating Wholeness: A Guide to Care and Counseling in Faith Communities*. New York: Continuum, 2001

Lartey, Emmanuel Y. *In Living Color: An Intercultural Approach to Pastoral Care and Counseling*, 2nd ed. London: Jessica Kingsley, 2003.

Lester, Andrew D. *Anger: Discovering Your Spiritual Ally*. Louisville: Westminster John Knox, 2007.

Liebert, Elizabeth. *The Soul of Discernment: A Spiritual Practice for Communities and Institutions*. Louisville: Westminster John Knox, 2015.

Linden, David J. *Touch: The Science of the Hand, Heart, and Mind*. New York: Penguin, 2016.

Luft, Joseph and Harry Ingham, "The Johari Window, a Graphic Model of Interpersonal Awareness." In *Proceedings of the Western Training Laboratory in Group Development*. Los Angeles: UCLA, 1955.

Macy, Joanna. *World as Lover, World as Self*. Berkeley: Parallax, 1991.

Malhotra, Rajiv. *Indra's Net*. San Francisco: HarperCollins, 2016.

Mayor, David and Marc S. Micozzi, ed. *Energy Medicine East and West: A Natural History of QI*. London: Churchhill Livingstone, 2011.

McFague, Sallie. *The Body of God: An Ecological Theology*. Minneapolis: Fortress, 1992.

Miller-McLemore, Bonnie. "Embodied Knowing, Embodied Theology: What Happened to the Body?" *Pastoral Psychology* 62, no. 5 (2013): 743–58.

Mitchell, Beverly Eileen. *Black Abolitionism: A Quest for Human Dignity*. Maryknoll, NY: Orbis, 2005.

Moltmann-Wendel, Elisabeth. *I Am My Body: A Theology of Embodiment*. New York: Continuum, 1995.

Montilla, R. Esteban and Ferney Medina. *Pastoral Care and Counseling with Latino/as*. Minneapolis: Augsburg Fortress, 2006.

Moreland-Capuia, Alisha. *Training for Change: Transforming Systems to be Trauma-Informed, Culturally Responsive, and Neuroscientifically Focused*. London: Springer Nature, 2019.

Moschella, Mary Clark. *Ethnography as a Pastoral Practice: An Introduction*. Cleveland: Pilgrim, 2008.

Nouwen, Henri J. M. *Life of the Beloved: Spiritual Living in a Secular World*. New York: Crossroad, 2002.

O'Day, Gail. "Gospel of John." In *Women's Bible Commentary*, 3rd ed. ed. Carol A. Newsom, Sharon H. Ringe, and Jacqueline E. Lapsley, pp. 517–30. Louisville: Westminster John Knox, 2012.

O'Donohue, John. *Anam Cara: A Book of Celtic Wisdom*. New York: Harper Perennial, 1998.

O'Mara, Shane. *In Praise of Walking: A New Scientific Exploration*. New York: W. W. Norton, 2020.

Oden, Amy. *Right Here Right Now: The Practice of Christian Mindfulness*. Nashville: Abingdon Press, 2017.

Oliver, Mary. "The Summer Day," In *New and Selected Poems*, vol. 1. Boston: Beacon, 1992.

_____. "Wild Geese." In *Dream Work*. New York: The Atlantic Monthly Press, 1986.

Packer, Toni. *The Silent Question: Meditating in the Stillness of Not-Knowing*. Boston: Shambhala, 2007.

Palmer, David A. *Qigong Fever: Body, Science, and Utopia in China*. New York: Columbia University Press, 2007.

Park, Andrew Sung. *From Hurt to Healing: A Theology of the Wounded*. Nashville: Abingdon Press, 2004.

Richardson, Ronald W. *Creating a Healthier Church*. Minneapolis: Augsburg Fortress, 1996.

Ruether, Rosemary Radford. "Re-evaluating the Body in Eco-Feminism." In *The Body and Religion*, ed. R. Ammicht Quinn and Elsa Tamez. London: SCM, 2002.

Rumi, Jalal al-Din Rumi. *The Essential Rumi*, trans. Coleman Barks. San Francisco: HarperOne, 1997.

Savage, John. *Listening and Caring Skills: A Guide for Groups and Leaders*. Nashville: Abingdon Press, 1996.

Schroeter, Vincentia. "Character Armoring: A Wall Between Oneself and the World." In *The Revelation of the Breath: A Tribute to Its Wisdom, Power, and Beauty*, ed. Sharon G. Mijares, pp. 71–82. Albany: SUNY Press, 2015.

Shufro, Cathy. "War and After: Veterans of Recent Conflicts Talk about Their Lives Before and After Deployment." *Yale Alumni Magazine* (May/June 2016).

Siegel, Allen M. *Heinz Kohut and the Psychology of the Self*. New York: Routledge, 1996.

Singleton, Mark. *Yoga Body: The Origins of Modern Posture Practice*. New York: Oxford University Press, 2010.

Sorajjakool, Siroj. *The Practice of Wu-wei, Negativity, and Depression: The Principle of Non-Trying in the Practice of Pastoral Care*. Binghamton, New York: Haworth, 2001.

Stairs, Jean. *Listening for the Soul: Pastoral Care and Spiritual Direction*. Minneapolis: Augsburg Fortress, 2000.

Stanley, Christopher D. *Hebrew Bible: A Comparative Approach*. Minneapolis: Fortress, 2010.

Steward, Anne W. "Eve and Her Interpreters." In *Women's Bible Commentary*, 3rd ed. Ed. Carol A. Newsom, Sharon H. Ringe, and Jacqueline E. Lapsley, pp. 232–42. Louisville: Westminster John Knox, 2012.

Swan, Liz Stillwaggon, ed. *Yoga Philosophy for Everyone: Bending Mind and Body*. West Sussex, UK: Wiley-Blackwell, 2012.

The Blue Cliff Record, trans. Thomas Cleary and J. C. Cleary. Boston: Shambhala, 1977.

The United Methodist Hymnal. Nashville: Abingdon Press, 1989.

Thurman, Howard. *The Inward Journey*. Richmond, IN: Friends United, 1961.

Tolle, Eckhart. *The Power of Now: A Guide to Spiritual Enlightenment*. Novato, CA: New World, 2004.

Trible, Phyllis. *Texts of Terror: Literary-Feminist Readings of Biblical Narratives*. Minneapolis: Fortress, 1984.

Turner, Victor. *The Ritual Process: Structure and Anti-Structure*. New York: Aldine de Gruyter, 1995.

Ulanov, Ann Belford. *Knots and their Untying: Essays on Psychological Dilemmas*. Einsiedein, Switzerland: Daimon Verlag, 2020.

Ulanov, Barry and Ann Belford. *Religion and the Unconscious*. Philadelphia: Westminster, 1975.

van der Kolk, Bessel. *The Body Keeps the Score: Brain, Mind, and Body in the Healing of Trauma*. New York: Penguin, 2014.

Walker-Barnes, Chanequa. *Too Heavy a Yoke: Black Women and the Burden of Strength*. Eugene, OR: Cascade, 2014.

Waters, Sonia A. *Addiction and Pastoral Care*. Grand Rapids: Wm. B. Eerdmans, 2019.

Weems, Lovett H. *Take the Next Step: Leading Lasting Change in the Church*. Nashville: Abingdon Press, 2003.

Wesley, Charles. "Hymn XL." In *Hymns for Children*. Bristol: E. Farley, 1763. Reprinted by Gale Eighteen Century Collections Online Print Editions.

Wimberly, Edward P. *Recalling Our Own Stories: Spiritual Renewal for Religious Caregivers*. Minneapolis: Fortress, 2019.

Winnicott, Donald Woods. *The Maturational Processes and the Facilitating Environment*. Madison, CT.: International Universities Press, 1988.

Wolterstoff, Nicholas. *Lament for a Son*. Grand Rapids: Wm. B. Eerdmans, 1987.

Yoder, Christine Roy. "Proverbs." In *Women's Bible Commentary*, 3rd ed. ed. Carol A. Newsom, Sharon H. Ringe, and Jacqueline E. Lapsley, pp. 232–42. Louisville: Westminster John Knox, 2012.

Yong, Amos. *The Bible, Disability, and the Church: A New Vision of the People of God*. Grand Rapids: Wm. B. Eerdmans, 2011.

SUBJECT INDEX

abuse, 4, 5n.9, 13, 51, 82, 133, 136, 151
acceptance, 25, 78, 97, 171
addiction, 46, 105, 153n.18
anger, 12–13, 27–28, 54–55, 62, 78, 89, 90, 110, 131, 147, 150, 154n.19; at injustice, 171
anxiety, 12, 38, 47–48, 50, 55, 57, 73, 79, 87, 100, 110, 132, 141, 145, 149, 159, 167, 171
armor, 124, 130–31, 134–36; as body protection, 124, 131; of God, 128, 133
authenticity, 19, 56, 93, 97
authority, 1, 107, 133
awareness, 3, 27, 30, 36, 44, 59, 67, 70, 72–76, 81, 95, 101, 107, 112–13, 134, 149, 151, 153, 166–68

baptism, 115
Bible studies, 51, 119
Black Lives Matter, 147, 172
blessing, 55, 74, 79, 107, 124, 164; and body senses, 91
Body Care Prayer: 8, 23, 41, 63, 79, 97, 121, 139, 159
body: definitions of, 6, 67; messages, 5, 29, 38–39, 142; presence, 52, 138, 150; senses, 78, 81–82, 86, 87–89, 91–92, 96–97; story, 9–10, 13–22, 43, 62, 69, 87, 90, 93, 150

boundaries, 27, 83, 85, 93
brain, 25n.1, 27–28, 44, 46, 54, 73, 83, 113, 149
breath practice, 112, 59, 96, 112, 167–69

caregiver, 3, 4, 16–17, 19, 21–22, 39, 53, 71, 74, 86–87, 90, 116, 126, 129, 137, 155n.22, 169
caregiving, 7, 16, 38, 85
children, 10, 27, 29, 61, 108, 131, 147–48, 151, 155n.22
community, 13, 17n.12, 32, 38, 63, 72, 74, 91, 107–8, 130, 153–54; care practices, 40–41, 54, 71, 75, 94, 119, 125, 134–36, 151–53, 169; as source of healing, 74; as the body of Christ, 157
compassion, 27, 50–51, 58, 63, 70, 77, 84n.9, 96, 108, 120, 125, 133, 139; as an attribute of God, 148; biblical words for, 58
conflict, 11–13, 48, 131, 141, 144, 157; in churches, 63n.30
contemplative practice, 6, 100–102, 104, 106, 108–11, 114–15, 156, 171
control, 16, 21, 49, 52–53, 61, 75, 138, 141, 155
counseling, 16, 30, 38, 40, 66, 111

Subject Index

covenant, 50, 53, 102-103, 105, 114–16, 124–25, 136, 146, 148–49, 164; God's, 71, 102, 114–15, 118, 148
CPE (Clinical Pastoral Education), 51n.14
creation, 10, 34, 43–45, 70, 75, 154, 159, 171; and care of, 29, 45, 93, 124, 127, 142, 165; delight in, 104, 154; as God's body, 46; order and rhythm of, 14–15, 26, 31, 35, 46
culture, 17n.12, 25, 78, 84, 123–24, 154, 158, 169, 172

depression, 89, 110n.20
defenses, 154, 169
denial, 153–54
disability, 9, 143n.6
discernment, 50, 107–8; definition of, 51
diversity, 101, 154, 156, 158–59
dream, 1,2, 8, 36, 40, 61, 163

empathy, 17, 22; definition of, 2
emotions, 12, 27–28, 31, 38–39, 43, 47–49, 52, 60, 66–68, 85, 87, 97, 100, 111–12, 120, 127, 131, 137, 139, 148, 171
Eucharist, 102

faith, 1–3, 9–10, 14, 20, 23, 31, 41, 51, 59, 70, 81–82, 91, 94, 105, 118, 120, 123, 126, 128–29, 136
fear, 2, 11–13, 21, 45, 48–50, 52, 55–57, 66, 70, 79, 81–82, 87, 100, 105, 114, 118, 139, 148, 156, 163, 167, 171–72
felt sense, 69–70, 75–77, 137; definition of, 76
focusing, 28, 30, 65–79; as community practice, 71–79
freedom, 2, 22, 57, 79, 109

gender, 17, 129, 141, 142, 144–45, 156, 163
gifts, 1, 22, 26, 95–97, 100, 106–7, 124
God, image of, 26, 41, 45, 51, 142
grace, 10–11, 13, 34, 85, 149; God's, 10, 14, 21, 55, 124
grief, 1–2, 31–32, 47, 52–53, 66, 87–90, 123–24, 147, 161

healing, 5–8, 14–16, 21, 25, 27, 53, 58, 72–75, 77, 81, 84, 87, 92, 96, 109, 113, 119, 131, 134, 136, 150, 164–65, 171; definitions of, 74
health, 15, 21, 41, 74, 111, 131, 161, 164–65, 172
honesty, 63, 153
hope, 2, 31–32, 44
hospitality, 19–20, 69, 91, 149
human dignity, 142–43, 146; and the *imago Dei*, 142n.2
humility, 20, 69–70, 93

"I-You," 33–35
identity, 1, 17, 22, 86, 95, 107, 109, 129n.9, 156, 164; of the church, 115, 153; as God-inspired, 1, 8, 124
inclusion, 148, 159, 172
interfaith, 119, 157
interpathy, 70

Jesus, 2, 14–15, 19, 22, 26–27, 30, 57–58, 82, 91, 94, 101, 109, 115, 123, 158, 166
justice, 2, 14, 22, 44, 102, 114, 127, 130, 133, 142–43, 146–48, 153, 159, 165–66, 172

labyrinth, 113, 166
laments, 22, 87, 95, 146
leadership, 78, 91, 132, 134, 151, 153, 170

liberation, 58
listening, 2, 20–21, 39, 69–70, 72, 86, 108, 116, 132–33, 149, 150–51, 154–55, 159, 168; with God, 103, 108; with the body, 2–3, 19, 50, 108, 112, 154, 159; as hospitality, 69–70
loss, 31, 47, 53, 90–91, 171
love, 3, 6, 10, 11–12, 23, 27–28, 32, 35, 47, 50, 58, 82, 85, 93–94, 97, 99, 101, 108, 111, 114–17, 124, 138–39, 157–59; care practices of, 138; of God, 45, 101, 110, 128, 148

marginalization, 82
medicine, 21, 113, 113n.27
meditation, 15, 36, 59, 100, 104, 106, 113, 116, 166–67, 171
metaphor, 6, 26n.2, 35, 66, 73, 77, 89, 129, 135–36, 143, 154, 156–57
mourning, 126
mutuality, 15, 27, 46, 62, 93, 103, 107, 157
myths, 155n.21

nature, 164–65
needs, 27, 44, 58, 62–63, 75, 85–86, 90, 107, 118–19, 145, 147

oppression, 79, 129, 142–43, 147

pain, 87–88, 94–95, 105, 110, 120, 124, 127, 132–33, 136–37, 151, 154, 159
paradox, 47, 55, 101
participant observation, 36, 38, 40
peace, 2, 11, 14, 31, 41, 63, 117, 128, 139, 172
platitudes, 170–71, 173
power, 6, 14, 34, 36, 45, 56, 69n.10, 101, 107, 129–30, 136, 139, 143, 147, 154, 157, 163; sharing of, 16, 74, 133; God's, 45, 118, 128, 139
prayer, 10, 15, 49, 60, 95, 99–101, 103–13, 116–17, 120
prophets, 53–54, 92

qigong, 113

monastic life, 103–4, 169

pastoral care, 7, 16, 51, 87, 151
psychiatrist, 12, 44, 155n.22
PTSD (post-traumatic stress disorder), 162. See also trauma

racism, 124, 142–43, 146–47
reactivity, 110, 155
reflection questions, 12–13, 15, 18, 22, 30, 32, 35, 37, 41, 46, 55, 65, 72, 75, 92, 106, 109, 135, 145, 153, 155
relationships, 14, 39, 48, 54, 61, 92–93, 105, 128–29, 132, 134, 139, 151, 157, 164; and care, 34, 51, 67, 85, 167; in early life and family, 4, 148–49, 151
relaxation response, 120

Sabbath, 14–15
sacrifice, 5
science, 40n.27, 44, 83, 113, 113n.6, 154
secrets, 142, 146–52, 154, 159; and community practices, 152–53
secure base, 88, 152, 155
self: -care, 125, 137; -discovery, 74; hood, 6; -image, 41, 74; -in-presence, 67
sexual orientation, 17, 135, 156
shame, 21–22, 27–28, 49, 135, 141–42, 144, 147–48, 155; positive and negative functions of, 27n.9

Subject Index

silence, 55–56, 100–103, 105–6, 108–9, 111, 119–20, 141; as a form of prayer, 99–104, 108–11, 118–19, 159; as negative, 22, 54, 102, 127, 141–42, 146–48, 151–54; as support for care, 105–6, 109–10, 119, 125, 138

small group exercise(s), 16, 90

Spirit, 14, 75, 92–93, 99, 101, 108, 113, 115, 128, 138, 157–59

spiritual care, 6, 16–19, 21, 34, 39, 51, 69, 100–101, 106, 108, 112, 124–25, 127, 167

spiritual director, 99, 105, 107, 162

stereotypes, 17, 135, 156

story, 2, 9–10, 12-13, 16, 18, 19, 21–22, 32, 37, 46, 62, 78, 93, 99, 120, 133, 143, 150, 153–54, 159, 163, 168; in the Bible, 5, 22, 188; God's, 12. See also body story

story lines, 12–13, 110

stress, 6, 39, 44, 52–53, 58, 60, 111, 119, 125–26, 132–33, 135, 162

suffering, 19, 21–22, 41, 52–53, 86, 105, 120, 146, 161–62

systems theory, 48

systemic inequality, 8

teaching, 3, 13, 27, 58, 61, 70, 116, 126, 143–45, 156, 158, 161, 165, 167, 171

therapy, 28, 40, 71, 111, 135; body senses and, 92; definition of, 78

triangulation, 38, 48

trauma, 4–6, 25n.1, 44n.3, 69, 82, 100, 123–39, 162; and biblical interpretation, 4–5, 129–30; definition of, 126; and EMDR therapy, 71n.17; and safe body care practices, 124–31, 138, 159; and stories of protective care, 132–37

tears, 17, 34, 48, 50, 65–66, 81, 87–90, 97, 110, 133, 141

trust, 3-5, 13, 38, 83, 90, 155; and care, 36, 51, 76, 102, 107–8, 111–12, 127, 152, 154, 170

unconscious, 26, 39, 41, 69, 110–12, 131, 152–53, 168

vulnerability, 20, 69, 93, 141, 156

walking, 35, 48, 89, 103, 106, 113, 158, 163

weeping, 50, 53, 93, 114, 120

white supremacy, 142–43, 146

wisdom, 93, 123, 130, 139, 158, 171; body as source of, 11, 19, 51, 66, 108, 159; in the Bible, 16, 164

worship, 32, 92, 103, 108, 145; bulletin, 41, 106; online, 171; resources for, 121n.43

yoga, 51, 59–60, 169–70; definition of, 59

youth, 20, 29, 44, 119

Zen, 34, 92, 101, 113, 116, 145, 171

SCRIPTURE INDEX

OLD TESTAMENT

Genesis
1:26..26
1:26-28.......................................26
2...93
2:2-3..15
2:7...............................3, 93, 112
2:18..93
16:1-6..4
21:8-21..4
22...5
33:3..93
33:4..93

Exodus
3:1-12..34
34:6-7..148

Deuteronomy
6:4..91

Judges
19...4

1 Samuel
10:1..91
10:9-10..92

2 Samuel
12:15..2

1 Kings
19:3..118

19:4..118
19:5-6..118
19:8..118
19:9..55
19:12..55
19:13..55

Psalms
22:14-15......................................89
34:8..91
42:3..87
46:4......................................150–51
46:10..171
55:4-8..49
55:12-14......................................49
56:8-11..
90
139:13-15....................................35
139:14..106

Proverbs
1-8....................................... 163-64

Isaiah
42:18..143
43:1-4...................................114–15

Jeremiah
8:18-19..53
9:1-2..50

Ezekiel
24: 15-16....................................53

Scripture Index

Micah
6:6 114

NEW TESTAMENT

Matthew
12:25 158

Mark
1:41 27
4:35-41 .... 15, 27
6:31 57
6:34 58
8:12 27
8:17 27
9:19 27
9:36 27
10:16 27
10:21 27

Luke
3:21-22 115

John
1:14 14
1:16 14
5:5 109
5:6 109

5:7 109
5:8 109
11:2 91
11:35 91

Acts
13:3 91

Romans
8:22-23 75

1 Corinthians
11:25 102
12:13 157
12:23-24 156
12:25-26 157
13:13 157

2 Corinthians
3:18 115

Ephesians
6:10-20 128

Hebrews
13:2 70

Revelation
21:5 70

Acknowledgments

I give thanks to:

- Wesley Theological Seminary and students in our educational programs whose insights and reflections shape my teaching.

- Colleagues in the Society of Biblical Literature and Society for Pastoral Theology whose scholarship informs my work.

- Denise Dombkowski Hopkins, colleague and friend, for her wisdom, encouragement, and editorial precision.

- Kevin North and Linda Hodson for moral support.

- Abingdon Press and its dedicated editorial team.